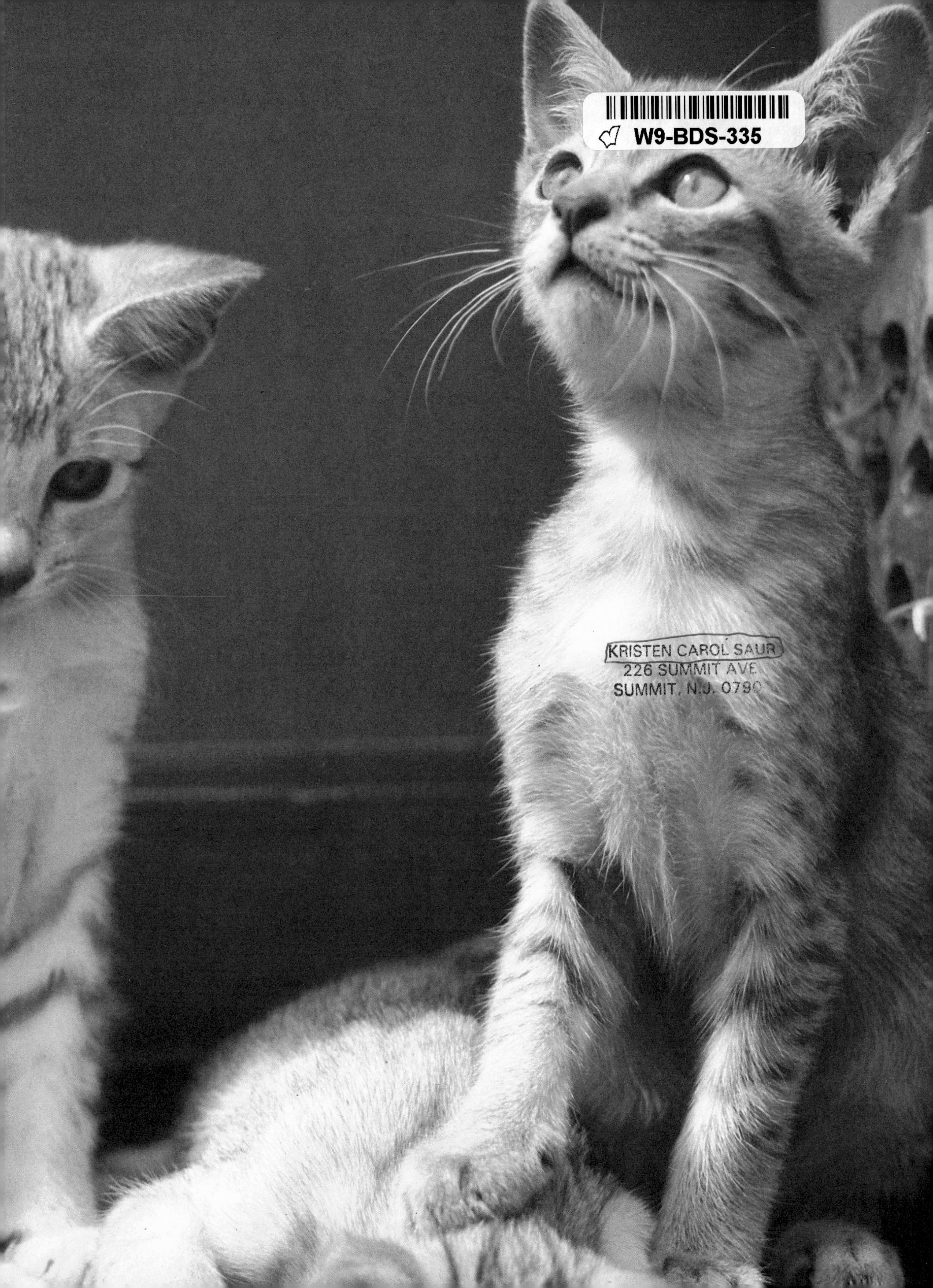

1989

Kristen,    Christmas.

Merry    Love,
              Dad

# The Complete Book of the
# CAT

# The Complete Book of the
# CAT

by Anna and Michael Sproule
Consultant Editor: Michael Findlay, BMVS, MRCVS, MIPR

## GALLERY BOOKS

An Imprint of W. H. Smith Publishers Inc.
112 Madison Avenue
New York City 10016

# CONTENTS

This book was devised and produced by
Multimedia Books Limited

**Editor: Richard Rosenfeld**
**Production: Arnon Orbach**
**Design: Behram Kapadia**
**Picture Research: Dee Robinson**
**Illustrations: Janos Marffy**

First published in the United States of America 1989 by
Gallery Books, an imprint of W.H. Smith Publishers Inc.,
112 Madison Avenue, New York, NY 10016.

ISBN 0 8317 1544 8

Origination by D.S. Colour International, London
Jacket originated by Reprocraft Studios (87) Limited
Printed in Italy by Imago Publishing Limited

*This page:* A beautifully marked
tabby cat licks its lips in
anticipation.

*Page 1:* Even this delicate-looking
ginger shorthair kitten shows the
teeth of a carnivore.

*Pages 2-3:* This long-haired tabby
has been imterrupted while
grooming herself in the garden.

# 1 CATS FROM THE BEGINNING

To find the true ancestor of today's domestic cat, we have to go back about 40 million years, roughly half-way in time between the extinction of the dinosaurs and the modern day.

The death of the reptilian dinosaurs, which had dominated the animal kingdom for some 120 million years, left mammals to carry on the main thrust of evolution on land. One of these primitive mammals was *Miacis*, which itself evolved into a number of successive groups. *Miacis* lived in the trees and was able to move freely among them in search of food. Its teeth were adapted for tearing and cutting flesh, and its agility made it a superb hunting animal – a born survivor in an age when creatures less viable were still dropping out of the evolutionary race.

The nearest relative to *Miacis* in the modern world is the civet, found in sub-tropical Africa and Asia.

*Left:* Morning in a summer meadow. Two little members of the latest generation of domestic cats explore their surroundings; behind them stretch millions of years of evolutionary history.

7

Evolution is a long story of mixed successes and failures, and although many of the descendants of *Miacis* were successful, some branches prospered better than others. Like the dinosaurs before them, members of the *Miacis* family spread rapidly across the world, with the exception of Australasia, adapting to the living conditions they found and to the prey that was available in their new territories as they colonized them.

By about 10 million years ago, two separate groups of descendants of *Miacis* could be distinguished; these were the *Hoplophoneus* group of large animals and the smaller *Dinictis*, though many of the latter group were large by comparison with the modern domestic cat.

*Hoplophoneus* was doomed to extinction. Its main feature was the development of so-called sabre teeth, with which it stabbed its prey before tearing it apart. One member of the group was *Smilodon* or the sabre-toothed tiger, a misleading name since it bore not even a passing resemblance to the tiger of today.

## On the attack

It was a particularly fearsome beast, with curved canine teeth 6 in (15 cm) long and jaws which could open to 90 degrees. Its prey were the large, lumbering grazing

*Above:* An artist's representation of a primitive sabre-toothed cat, *Dinictis felina*, based on remains that date from the Oligocene period.

animals that lived on the great plains and at the forest edge. Prey was abundant and therefore no great skill was required to track down and kill the grazers.

As the supply of grazing animals diminished, and some of them, such as the early ancestors of the gazelle and the antelope, developed the ability to escape from a predator at high speed, *Smilodon* and the other *Hoplophoneus* groups were, quite literally, left behind. Failing to adapt, they became extinct – but only after a long period of success. The earliest members of the group are believed to have emerged about 35 million years ago, and it has been claimed that sabre-tooth remains found in California date from only about 13 000 years ago.

The *Dinictis* group, better able to adapt to changing conditions, was more successful, and it is from this that all the members of the "cat family", from the lion to the domestic cat, are descended. The group was at one time almost 100 species strong, and about one third of these have survived in modern forms.

## Tree hunters

*Dinictis*, needing to work harder for its living in a changing world, nurtured and developed its hunting skills. When the easier prey, such as grazing animals, was in short supply – the number of grazers fluctuated enormously with climatic changes – *Dinictis* took to hunting in the trees, aided by its sharp claws. Tree-dwelling creatures were more evasive than ground-living prey, so *Dinictis* had to sharpen its senses to feed.

Above all, most species developed the retractable claw, a feature which is characteristic of the domestic cat and which enabled them to add speed and accuracy of movement of while retaining the ability to tear at the flesh of their victims. This claw gave them a lead in the survival stakes, and it may be due to this ingenious evolutionary invention that we are able today to enjoy the company of our own cats as well as to marvel at the ferocity of the tiger, the majesty of the lion and the treacherous grace of the leopard.

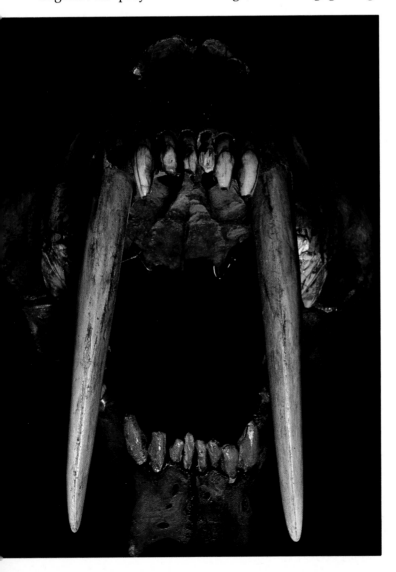

*Left:* The awe-inspiring gape of prehistory's *Smilodon*, also known as the sabre-toothed cat. To accommodate the huge canines, its jaws could open at right angles to each other.

*Right:* The ultimate prehistoric ancestor of all cats was *Miacis*, a slender animal with a pointed snout. This modern civet is also a *Miacis* descendant, and the cat's distant cousin.

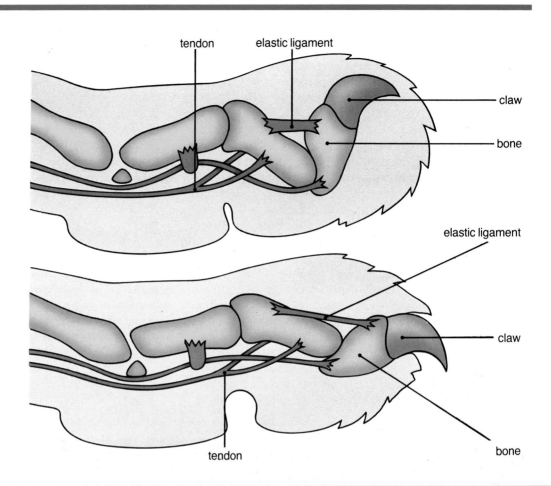

*Right:* The key to feline success? The cat's power to retract its claws is one of the outstanding characteristics of the whole family. Only the cheetah, which relies on speed rather than stealth to catch its prey, does not possess claws that pull back into the toes. Claws protected in this way stay permanently sharp and ready for use; in addition, the sheathing mechanism – shown here – allows the cat to walk and run much more quietly than an animal whose claws are permanently extended.

tendon

elastic ligament

claw

bone

elastic ligament

claw

tendon

bone

From the shifts and changes of evolution, slightly less than 40 (experts do not agree on the exact number) different species have emerged to form the three groups that make up the zoological cat family of today. Interestingly, though, they range from, at one extreme, the tiger (*Panthera tigris*), which can weigh up to 800 lb (360 kg), to, at the other, the tiny Rusty-spotted cat (*Felis rubiginosus*) of southern India, which weighs in at a mere 3-4 lb (1.6 kg).

Your own domestic cat may well, at one time or another, display the characteristic facial expression of a lion, the balancing act of such tree-cats as the ocelot, and a turn of speed reminiscent of the cheetah – thus demonstrating that it has links with each of the three groups which make up the cat family.

## Species

Your cat is, in fact, a member of the genus *Felis,* which includes nearly 30 species of "small cats" as well as the puma (*F. concolor*). The domestic cat, *Felis catus,* is recognized by zoologists as a species in its own right. Some species, such as the African golden cat (*F. aurata*) and the Borneo bay cat (*F. badia*), have a very limited distribution. It is mainly because of these small, isolated species that arguments over the exact number of species of cat have arisen.

Larger than *Felis,* but only six in number, are members of the genus *Panthera,* the kings of the cat world, led by the tiger and the lion. They make up a list of some of the most feared and ferocious beasts known to man: the tiger, the lion, the leopard and the jaguar, together with the clouded leopard and the snow leopard. The *Panthera* group contains the great roarers and, as one would expect, they have highly developed vocal apparatus. Sadly, today, many of the *Panthera* are classed as endangered, including the tiger (down to about 2500 in the wild), the snow leopard (number of survivors unknown) and the Asiatic lion (perhaps about 300 survivors). The fur trade and loss of natural habitat have also contributed to the decline of both the jaguar and the leopard.

The cheetah, of the genus *Acinonyx,* is unique among cats in having non-retractable claws. This handsome cat is second only to the domestic cat in its historical relationship with man, trained for its speed and hunting skill by the ancient Egyptians and, until recently, by the princes of India. It has been timed over short distances at 70 mph (112 kph), though about 50 mph (80 kph) is more usual. The cheetah also has an extremely fast acceleration rate, taking just a few seconds from rest to a speed of 40 mph (64 kph), as fast as – if not faster than – the average sports car.

*Right:* A cheetah at full sprint closes on its prey. Going all out, it can reach speeds of up to 70 mph (112 kph), although it cannot keep up such a surge of power for long. Its non-retractable claws help it grip the ground firmly, while the long tail acts as a rudder, improving balance and cornering skills at speed.

*Right:* One of the smallest of the modern cat family, this Little Spotted Cat or Oncilla is native to Central and South America.

*Left:* Although the lion can come close to it in size, the tiger is the biggest cat of all. Its stripes help it blend with the shadows thrown by foliage in its preferred habitats.

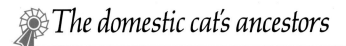

The first conclusive evidence we have of the domestication of the cat comes from the civilization of ancient Egypt, dating around about 2000 BC. Earlier than that, any attempt to trace the process by which various species of wild cat came to be adopted by man can be only, at best, informed guesswork. Certainly, ancient Egypt was not the first society based on agriculture, and any grain-growing community needs protection against the depredations of rats and mice. It would not be surprising to hear that cats were known in the farming villages of Anatolia in 8000 BC or of Mesopotamia 4000 years later. However, we can only speculate on that, noting at the same time that other creatures such as weasels and ferrets were also available as pest controllers.

## Mummified remains

The clues we have to the origin of the domestic cat come from the mummified bodies of ancient Egyptian cats compared with two species of true wild cats. This shows that among Egyptian cats a type related to the African wild cat (*Felis lybica* or *libyca*) was most prominent. This is a tabby with a sandy color and less defined markings than the familiar tabbies of today. It is a species native to the Middle East, Africa and Mediterranean Europe, and it is reasonable to suppose that it would have been tempted to take advantage of the comfort and hunting possibilities of Egyptian homes and farms.

As cat owners know to their chagrin – and sometimes to their renewed pleasure – cats are opportunists, capable of becoming independent for a period and returning home when the mood takes them. So it is perfectly possible to imagine populations of *F. lybica* moving between a domesticated and semi-wild state, possibly interbreeding with other species in the meantime. This would explain the additional presence among mummified Egyptian cats of examples of the ring-tailed jungle cat *Felis chaus*.

*Above:* The cat that started it all. A modern African Wild Cat (*Felis lybica*) takes the sun. The tabby markings are present, though less distinct than in the domestic cat. The ears are noticeably larger.

*Left:* Some of the Egyptian cat mummies that have been found contained cats that looked like this Jungle Cat (*Felis chaus*). So this is probably another of the domestic cat's ancestors.

*Right:* The third partner in the domestic cat's make-up. The European Wild Cat (*Felis silvestris*) has stronger tabby markings than the African Wild Cat, and is closer to our pet cats in its build.

## The European wild cat

With the spread of the Egyptian-domesticated *lybica* through Europe, a third ancestor *F. silvestris*, the European wild cat, makes an appearance. This is a black-striped tabby whose tail ends in a rounded black tip. Expert opinion differs on the significance of *F. silvestris* in the "mix" making up the modern domestic cat. It is difficult to imagine *F. silvestris*, with its wild, virtually untameable nature, actually approaching and living happily alongside human settlements as *F. lybica* evidently did in Egypt. However, interbreeding no doubt took place between *lybica*, as it spread, and *silvestris*, and this would have had the effect of bringing the black of the tabby markings into greater prominence. There may also have been natural darkening of *lybica*'s coat in northern Europe in response to climatic changes.

But the mix is not yet complete. We have also to add Pallas's cat (*F. manul*) from central Asia. According to some, the *manul* could have contributed the long fur to the earliest forerunners of today's Persians, although it is also argued that this was the result of a genetic mutation originating in central Asia.

## Interbreeding

It is important to remember that the interbreeding of wild cat species was not an isolated affair, but a continuous chain of events: domestic cat with semi-tame wild cat, semi-tame with natural wild cat, feral (escaped domestic) cat with wild cat, and so on. Probably the closest we can come to the truth is to say that there are undoubtedly elements of *lybica*, *chaus*, *silvestris* and perhaps *manul* in the domestic cats of today.

# Egyptian and European cats

From Egyptian arts and crafts we have a record of the significant part played in ancient Egyptian life by the cat as hunter, retriever, pet and ultimately goddess. By about 1900 BC cats were being used by hunters, and by about 500 years later they had become associated with the love-goddess Pasht (otherwise known as Bast, Bastet, Ubasti or Oubastis). Our word "puss" is said to be derived from "Pasht", but this may well be no more than guesswork.

The temple of Pasht was at Bubastis, about half-way between the present city of Cairo and the Mediterranean coast, and a great festival in honor of Pasht was held each year. The great temple statue of Pasht was only one of many hundreds of representations of the goddess, used for personal and domestic worship and often cast in bronze, showing a cat-headed woman, sometimes with four kittens as attendants.

## Cat cemeteries

The Egyptians mummified the bodies of their dead cats and placed them in specially-constructed cemeteries in cat-shaped wooden or bronze caskets. As many as 300000 cat mummies were found at one site, Beni Hassan, in the nineteenth century. Not realizing their significance, the excavators sold almost all the relics to be crushed for bonemeal. The physical characteristics of the Egyptian domestic cat have been deduced from the relatively small number of mummies that escaped this ignominious and wasteful end.

Although the Egyptians discouraged the export of cats, some were probably taken to Italy by traders, or perhaps stowed away on merchant ships. The citizens of Imperial Rome gave cats a welcome, and the Roman legions took cats with them on their campaigns, presumably to help guard their stores, while Roman colonial households included cats among quite a menagerie of family pets. Over the next few centuries, the cat became cherished as a companion among the people of Europe as well as valued as a pest-destroyer. Cats also found homes in monasteries and nunneries, where they were allowed as pets although their fur was also prescribed for clerical dress. As this instruction was intended to reflect the vow of poverty, it suggests that there was no commercial trade in cat pelts.

There is also some evidence that the cat became the favored pet of the European intelligentsia, including the fourteenth-century Italian poet Petrarch. European cat-lovers by this time had something new to delight them, for the Crusaders had brought back from their travels the first long-hairs.

*Left:* A cat mummy from Ancient Egypt. With its wrappings and wooden funeral mask, it has been made in the same way as the much more costly mummies of Egyptian royalty, and for the same reason: to show honor to the dead.

There was now, however, more serious work for the cat to do. In 1348, the Black Death – bubonic plague, carried by a flea that lived in the coat of the black rat – reached northern Europe, killing off one in four of the population and bringing economic as well as human disaster. It was a matter of common, though not yet scientific, observation that the plague of black rats coincided with the spread of the Black Death, and cats, whose popularity had been waning, were hastily (though not hastily enough) brought in to fight the disease-carriers.

*Below:* In this 3000-year-old painting of the Egyptian gods, a sacred cat cuts off the head of the evil serpent that threatened to destroy the sun.

*Right:* Two domestic tabbies of early medieval times, as shown by a European monk in a drawing of Adam giving names to all the animals.

*Above:* A modern Western member of a very old Eastern breed: the Korat, named after the province of Thailand from which it originally came.

*Left:* In this ancient painting of Thai breeds, the Siamese can be clearly seen at the top right. The blue Korat is bottom left.

When the cat reached China – the date is uncertain, but there were probably domesticated cats in China by the time of Christ – we begin to hear tales of its baleful influence and, in particular, of the bad luck brought by the sight of a black cat. (This is a world-wide superstition, the English being unusual in regarding a black cat as a sign of *good* luck.) Ancient Chinese civilization seems to have been suspicious of cats, which were thought to bring poverty. This may have extended from the thought that a home or farm where a cat was needed to destroy vermin could not be a prosperous, well-organized one. The presence of a cat would thus be a negative status symbol.

One way of avoiding the misfortune of poverty was to station a china figure of a cat, seated and alert, in a suitable place of prominence. Presumably the same motive inspired the pictures of cats which graced the walls of many Chinese houses. Perhaps not too much significance should be attached to the ambivalence of the ancient Chinese view of cats; quite probably society was simply divided, as ours is, into those who love cats and those who regard them with at least suspicion, if not outright distaste.

## Saving the silk farms

In India the cat was more fortunate, and indeed there was a cat goddess associated, like the Egyptian Pasht, with maternity, among other things. The Japanese, too, became ardent cat lovers, initially because their silk farms were infested with mice. In a slightly later period, around 1000 AD, pet cats became fashionable playthings in the home, to which they were often confined by silken leashes. This delighted the silk farm mice, which prospered to the point where the industry was threatened with disaster. The Japanese therefore adopted the Chinese custom of painting cat pictures on their walls to discourage the mice, but ultimately the Emperor ordered cats to be freed so that they could return to their duties on the farms. The bobtail cat is Japan's distinctive contribution to the feline world. It is not known when it first appeared, but it has certainly existed in Japan – virtually unknown to outsiders until a couple of generations ago – for many centuries.

The religions of the East echoed Egypt in adopting the cat as a mystic symbol. The Hindus regarded the care of cats as a sacred duty, and the cat found its way, too, into the temples of Buddha, perhaps because of its meditative postures. The body of a cat, in Buddhist lore, is the temporary resting-place of the soul of exceptionally spiritual people.

In the West, the most celebrated Far Eastern cats are, of course, the Siamese. Not all cats kept in Siam, as Thailand was then called, were the familiar seal points, though it does appear that that country was probably the true origin of the breed. Siamese cats are shown in the fourteenth-century Thai manuscript of *Cat-Book Poems*, though it was not until the nineteenth century that examples reached the West.

*Below:* In the West, cats by tradition do not have ghosts. But, as this Japanese print shows, Far Eastern cats are believed to have the power to turn into super-ghosts when they die.

From about 1400, in Europe, the cat entered its dark age, a period of persecution and cruelty fostered and sustained by the Roman church and continued by the Protestant churches of the Reformation. The basis of Christian animosity towards cats came from two separate sources.

One was the Norse cult, enjoying a revival in northern Europe about this time, of Freya, a love goddess who shared many of the characteristics of the ancient Egyptian Pasht. Among her specialities, however, was that Freya's chariot was drawn by cats. In the re-enactment of Freya's ride which was part of the revived pagan rituals, the chariot was drawn by young men. They drew her round her domain and then back to her secret temple, where they were ritually killed so that its location could not be revealed. But the cat association was enough to provide the cue for a religious assault on the species which was to last for at least 300 years.

## Witchcraft

The other stimulus was the association of cats with witchcraft. Not only was a cat often a witch's "familiar", her private link with the devil, but it was also believed that witches could change themselves into cats and back again at will. In the 1400s, Pope Innocent VIII issued instructions that when witches were burned their cats were to be burned also. In a superstitious society, it rapidly became impossible to be sure whether a cat was a real cat or a witch in disguise. Some witches were said

*Above:* Two witches and their cat familiars, as seen by a wood-engraver of the early seventeenth century. The striped tail shows that the cat on the broom stick is definitely a tabby.

to allow their cats to suck their blood, and so cats became attached, too, to the vampire legend. (It was not until Bram Stoker wrote *Dracula* late in the nineteenth century that the connection between vampires and bats, on the other hand, was born.)

Although the age of the cat's persecution eventually passed, it left behind a legacy of superstitions, some of which remain with us today.

The alleged unluckiness of black cats is one; witches were said to favor them. Another is the collection of old wives tales about cats and babies. The fear that a cat might smother a baby has provided a market for manufacturers of nets for baby carriages, but reported cases are extremely rare. The old wives have also been said to allege that a cat will kill a baby by "sucking its breath" or even – clearly a remnant of the witch-vampire story – sucking its blood. Another obvious survival of the witch association is the belief in Dorset, England, within living memory that girls who were fond of cats would die old maids.

Perhaps also because of the witchcraft link, cats feature in a number of folklore sayings about the weather. According to one of these, cats stop playing and compose themselves when rain is coming. Another says that rain is forecast if, when washing, a cat pays particular attention to the area over its ears.

In one notable respect, however, man's superstitions seem to have left the cat alone: in the matter of ghosts. Ghost lore is full of stories of spectral dogs, horses, birds and even cattle, but who ever heard of a ghost cat? Indeed, there is a Scottish Gaelic saying that as cats have nine lives, they live them all to the full in this world and so have no ghosts.

*Left:* The Norse goddess Freya, with her chariot and cats. It was partly the revival of her cult that spurred the Christian church on to its prolonged campaign of cat persecution during the fifteenth to eighteenth centuries.

*Right:* Witch's kitten? This little domestic black seems well aware of the dangers of the highly poisonous toadstools round it. In many places (though not the UK) black cats are often still thought of as unlucky.

When, in the eighteenth century, the Church began to lose its grip on European society, and became more concerned with its own divisions than with the threat of paganism or witchcraft from outside, the cat came slowly back into favor.

In intellectual circles in both France and England, cats were much prized as pets and began to be featured as such in paintings by, among others, Perroneau and Chardin. Also in France, François de Moncrif wrote an appreciative book about cats, and Charles Perrault's first printed version of the folk-tale *Puss in Boots,* which had appeared in 1697, was popular. In England, the eighteenth-century writer and critic Samuel Johnson kept a much-loved cat, Hodge. Johnson's biographer James Boswell gives this affectionate picture of Johnson and Hodge:

*"I shall never forget the indulgence with which he treated Hodge, his cat; for whom he himself used to go out and buy oysters, lest the servants having that trouble should take a dislike to the poor creature. I recollect Hodge one day scrambling up Dr. Johnson's breast apparently with much satisfaction, while my friend, smiling and half-whistling, rubbed down his back, and pulled him by the tail; and when I observed he was a fine cat, saying, 'Why, yes, Sir, but I have had cats whom I liked better than this'; and then, as if perceiving Hodge to be out of countenance, adding, 'but he is a very fine cat, a very fine cat indeed'."*

## Plague prevention

It was no coincidence that the upsurge in popularity of cats came at about the same time as the arrival in Europe of the brown rat, which migrated from central Asia in the early eighteenth century and reached Britain in 1730. Larger than the black rat, and fiercer, it quickly began to take over from its rival as it increased in numbers. Like the black variety, it was a potential plague-carrier, and it brought panic to Europe in case the great plagues of the seventeenth century should be repeated. In fact, and probably thanks to the cat, this did not happen.

In a society where household garbage was simply thrown into the street and left to rot, and where sewers, where they existed at all, were merely open drainage channels, cats were essential if humanity was not to be overwhelmed by the rat. Even the Comte de Buffon, a French writer on natural history who described the cat as treacherous, perverse, thieving and cunning, had to accept the realities of life. "The cat is an unfaithful domestic," he wrote in 1756, "and kept only from necessity in order to suppress a less domestic and more unpleasant animal."

He probably reflects the attitudes of his time in respecting cats more as ratters than as pets; the keeping of cats as household pets seems, in Europe, to have been confined to the upper and intellectual classes until well into the nineteenth century. But with the intervention of the brown rat, the cat's long night was over.

*Above:* In a sudden headlong pounce, this cat displays a fiendishly cunning and ruthless style of hunting.

*Right:* The cause of the cat's reinstatement in public favor. These modern brown rats are just as destructive as their ancestors of the eighteenth century.

*Left:* This keen fisherman appears in an eighteenth century portrait as an endearing pun on the human subject's name: Kitty Fisher. By this time, cats were clearly back in society's favor.

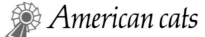

# American cats

It would be surprising if, given the number of *Felis* species indigenous to the Americas, no attempt was made in pre-colonial times to tame and breed from, say, the ocelot, the tiger cat or the jaguarundi a domestic, or at least a hunting or vermin-catching cat. But there is no hard evidence on this, only vague suppositions about the Aztecs, who may have kept a now-extinct breed of hairless cats, and stories drawn from Indian folklore.

It is known, however, that among the complement of about 100 souls on board the *Mayflower* there was at least one cat, together with a variety of other livestock such as pigs, poultry and goats. Bearing in mind the damage that vermin could do to stores, and the kind of settlement that the *Mayflower* pilgrims expected to set up, it would be natural for them to take the simple precaution of establishing a cat colony.

No doubt more cats arrived on the ships of the later settlers, and once regular trading began there would be occasional escapes of ships' cats to enrich the American feline stock. As the pioneers migrated into the interior of New England, into Canada, and ultimately to the West, they took cats with them, in some cases, no doubt, as treasured family pets, but mainly as extremely useful working animals.

*Above:* The essence of feline America. This American Shorthair is a natural US breed.

*Below:* In the US, she's called a calico; elsewhere, she's a tortoiseshell-and-white.

## Natural breeds

The harsh conditions and the extremes of the continental North American climate bred in cats, as in their owners, a peculiar ruggedness and toughness. This is apparent in the two natural American breeds, the American Shorthair and the Maine Coon.

There are few longhairs as tough as the Maine Coon, a breed said to have developed in the eighteenth century from longhairs brought over to New England by sailors and interbred with the already established domestics. It was the Maine Coon, groomed for stardom, that helped to get the cat fancy established in the United States, and the first shows featured the breed strongly. With the arrival from European breeders, late in the nineteenth century, of Persians, Russian Blues, Abyssinians and Siamese, however, the poor old Maine Coon, which had served US cat-lovers so well, fell out of favor as a show cat, though it continued to be valued as a family pet throughout the north-eastern states in particular. In show terms, the progress of the American Shorthair, too, was slow in the face of competition from more exotic imported breeds.

The cat fancy in the United States is generally reckoned to have taken off with the Madison Square Gardens Show of 1895, just as the British fancy dates its history from the 1871 Crystal Palace Show in London. But in America, as in Britain, it was not long before cat fanciers broke ranks and rival factions were set up. In Britain the divisions, which performed no service at all to the long-term interests of breeders, were finally resolved in 1910 with the establishment of one regulating body for breeding and showing, the Governing Council of the Cat Fancy. In the United States, the breakaway of the Cat Fanciers' Association in 1906 from the American Cat Association was followed by the creation of other groups, producing a multiple registration problem for US breeders which has not yet been resolved, and which leads some of them to cast envious glances across the Atlantic to Britain's single, definitive cat fancy body, the GCCF. There is now a rival breakaway group trying to establish itself in the UK, namely The Cat Association of Britain (CAB).

*Below:* Massive and densely furred, a brown tabby Maine Coon waits for admiration. The big ears are a characteristic mark of distinction.

A SOCIETY PUSS.

On a July day in 1871, the first British Cat Show, and indeed the first cat show in the world, was held at the Crystal Palace exhibition center on the heights overlooking south London. It was the brain-child of the artist and writer Harrison Weir, a now virtually forgotten figure who however deserves a tribute here, as in any book about cats, as one of the first people to understand both cats and the infinite pleasure to be gained from breeding and showing them.

His object in organizing the 1871 Show, he wrote, was "that the different breeds, colors, markings, etc. might be more carefully attended to, and the domestic cat, sitting in front of the fire, would then possess a beauty and an attractiveness to its owner unobserved and unknown, because uncultivated, before."

## Guide to breeding and showing

The National Cat Club of Great Britain was founded sixteen years later, with Harrison Weir as its first President; but, alas, he found that his ideal of a community of show cats and domestic cats could not be attained, and, finding that the Cat Club members were more interested in winning prizes than in cat welfare, he soon resigned. He was, however, the author of the first comprehensive guide to breeding and showing.

There was a world of difference between the rough ratcatcher of the city streets and the dockyards, and the carefully-groomed cats presented to the judges at the Crystal Palace. The ratcatchers, of course, continued at their work, but their sleeker cousins set about establishing themselves among their rich patrons. When and how did this transformation come about?

It is possible to pinpoint almost precisely the turning-point, at least in Britain, when cats ceased to be regarded with reluctant respect and came to be loved as pets among a wider audience.

In 1865, the Oxford don Lewis Carroll published *Alice's Adventures in Wonderland,* in which the Cheshire Cat was a gargoyle figure whose famous smile, in the original Tenniel illustrations, showed a number of sharp teeth. He was an object of respect, but far from lovable. Lewis Carroll's sequel, *Alice Through the Looking-Glass,* was begun three years later but not published until Christmas 1871, after the first Cat Show. Here, the mother cat, Dinah, and the two kittens Snowdrop and Kitty, are sympathetic figures – indeed, the mainsprings of the plot – and their role is distinctly as pets.

The two *Alice* books were, of course, enormously influential. Only after 1871, when children's reading primers were produced in large numbers in response to the introduction in England and Wales of compulsory primary education, did children's books begin to represent cats and kittens as lovable creatures suitable for little girls to play with, as in illustrations to, for example, the nursery-rhyme *Pussy-cat, pussy-cat, where have you been?*

It was Harrison Weir who first laid down standards for cat varieties and so stimulated interest in breeding. He was not a biologist, and some of his classifications have since been challenged. Nonetheless, he virtually single-handedly created what is known in Britain as "the cat fancy". But the final seal of approval for the ownership of cats was given when it was made known that Queen Victoria possessed a pair of blue Persians. At that point, the cat may truly be said to have arrived.

*Right:* This modern cat show is much bigger than the one organized by pioneer Harrison Weir, but the aim is the same: to find and reward feline beauty wherever it occurs.

*Left:* By the nineteenth century, cats were full members of polite society, and accepted as much-loved pets. "Society Puss" featured on a greetings card.

# 2 BASIC BIOLOGY

You have only to observe a cat – any cat – for a short while to see what a perfect machine it is for hunting. Its retractable claws enable it to run fast when required, with claws sheathed, and then to extend the claws for the kill. Its tail helps it to balance when leaping or climbing. To these bodily attributes are added a superb set of senses: eyes that are effective in dim light, highly discriminatory hearing and, for moving through confined spaces, sensitive whiskers.

The appreciation that cats are natural hunters is vital for anyone who really wants to understand them. However regularly its favorite food and tidbits are provided, its instincts will not allow the cat to forget that its ancestors had to find their own. It is interesting that, while breeding over many centuries has bred out the pack and hunting instincts in many dogs, this has never happened with even the most pampered breeds of cats.

## Natural hunters
The significance of this is that cats must be provided by their owners with either facilities or substitutes for exercising their hunting skills. Of course, this is not to say that no one should own a cat who does not also own half a forest for it to hunt in. One of the cat's most notable characteristics is its ability to adapt, and it has been spectacularly successful at that in urban areas, even without human support, as the number of stray and feral cats testifies. For an apartment-dwelling cat (and indeed for any cat's indoor sport) an empty spool of cotton, a screw of paper, a table-tennis ball or a felt toy (perhaps stuffed with dried catmint) provide excellent hunting and killing practice.

*Left:* With a powerful thrust of his strong back legs, this hunting cat launches himself into space. His eyes are firmly fixed on the point where he will land – safely.

*Above:* Early morning stretch. Only the tail tip is relaxed; most other parts of this kitten are getting a full work-out.

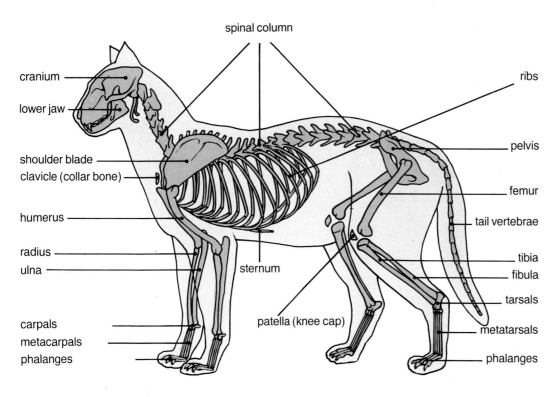

- spinal column
- cranium
- lower jaw
- shoulder blade
- clavicle (collar bone)
- humerus
- radius
- ulna
- carpals
- metacarpals
- phalanges
- sternum
- patella (knee cap)
- ribs
- pelvis
- femur
- tail vertebrae
- tibia
- fibula
- tarsals
- metatarsals
- phalanges

*Left:* The framework under the fur. As the diagram shows, the cat's feet are in fact its toes; the part corresponding to the human foot or hand forms the lower part of the feline leg.

Although there are some variations between different breeds, the basic body structure or "conformation" of cats is more similar across the whole species of *Felis catus* than is the case with dogs. This may well be because all cats, however domesticated and even cossetted, retain their hunting instinct; whereas the dog's relationship with man extends much further back into prehistory, and the breeding of dogs for a wider range of activities such as guarding, retrieving and guiding has encouraged the development of suitable characteristics and the suppression, or breeding out, of others.

A cat's limbs are operated by a complex system of levers activated by highly developed and precisely controllable muscles. The exceptional mobility of the cat's forequarters is made possible by the first joint of the front limbs, which lies directly between upper bone and shoulder-blade; there is no true collar-bone, as in the human skeleton, and so the forelimbs have a greater flexibility of movement.

## Circulation

While the cat's blood circulation system is broadly similar to that of other mammals, it is adapted to meet the needs of sudden changes from rest to extreme activity. For this reason, a cat's health is particularly closely related to the condition of its blood and circulatory system. The cat's normal heartbeat is 110-140 per minute, roughly twice the human rate, and at rest it breathes 30-50 times a minute, about four times as fast as man.

The normal temperature is 101.5°F (38.6°C). Although there are sweat glands in the cat's skin which dispose of impurities in the system, and whose most marked function is their use in marking territory by rubbing, the cat loses heat only through the sweat glands on its foot pads and through the mouth. The fur acts as insulator in hot and cold weather alike, however, and a peculiarity of cats familiar to many owners is their ability to withstand, and indeed enjoy, quite hot conditions.

## Feeding

A cat feeds by tearing pieces from its prey and swallowing them whole. This contrasts with the behavior of dogs, which normally chew their food to break it down partially before it enters the stomach. An adult cat has thirty teeth, with four prominent canines. These adult teeth – kittens have four less – are normally erupted by the age of seven months. In cats, the function of saliva is to "wash the food down" rather than start the digestion process, which is carried out by exceptionally strong digestive juices in the stomach and small intestine.

*Right:* A remarkable sequence of pictures that shows the cat's 'famous self-righting mechanism at work. A split second after the fall starts, the cat's spine is twisting; a split second more, and the cat is falling the right way up, legs extended to help soften its landing, which is on all four feet.

*I love little Pussy, her coat is so warm*, goes the old nursery rhyme, reminding us of the cat's most notable, and to many owners its most admirable, feature. For practical purposes, the different components of the coat can be divided into four: the guard hairs, the middle-length awn hairs, the softer under-hair, and the whiskers.

The guard hairs make up the generally rugged outer coat. Each hair is rooted in an individual follicle in the skin, and each follicle can react in response to signals in the nervous system. This reaction enables the cat to fluff out its coat in the cold, and, when in danger or facing a challenge, to make itself look more threatening.

The intermediate awn hairs are of more irregular length and structure. Some biologists do not regard them as a distinctive type from the guard and the down hairs, and therefore refer only to primary (guard) and secondary (down) hairs. The layer of hair closest to the skin is made up of soft, fluffy hair (lagunal hair) which grows in tufts from single follicles.

## Survival mechanism

Finally, the whiskers (or, to the biologist, the *vibrissae*) are found on the face and, in most cats, on the back of the forelegs. These are essential parts of the cat's survival mechanism, and any loss – for example, in a fight – severely curtails the ability to move about with confidence and to hunt with speed and accuracy.

It is thought that the whiskers on the forelegs are the feature that enables the cat to move so silently; the contact made, on taking a step forward, by the sensitive, foreleg whiskers can be likened to the scouting trick of putting the leading foot down brushingly before allow-

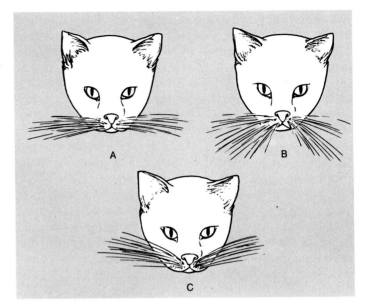

*Above:* The cat holds its whiskers in different positions for different things: A when at rest, B while walking, and C when sniffing, biting or on the defensive.

ing it to carry any weight. Facial whiskers, in addition to acting as width gauges and general indicators of the environment, also play a part in the communication between cats.

There are some exceptions to this general description of the cat's coat. The most notable is the Sphinx, bred from a mutated kitten in Canada in the 1960s, which is hairless except for whiskers. It remains to be seen whether the Sphinx will achieve widespread recognition as a pedigree breed, or whether it will survive only as a feline curiosity. The other exceptions are the Rex breeds, also derived from mutations, and also of fairly recent origin. The coat of the Cornish Rex has no guard hairs at all, and in the coat of the Devon Rex they are very short and waved.

## Grooming

Cats will attend efficiently to the care of their own coats for normal everyday purposes (though not to show standards) using their extremely flexible necks and shoulders. The natural spring and fall molts normally occur with no difficulties and often with little obvious sign, especially now that central heating has reduced the extremes of the domestic cat's living conditions and so tends to even out the loss of hair over the seasons. Because of the care that cats normally give to their coats in extended grooming sessions, any sign of abnormality, whether it be excessive dandruff or the appearance of thin areas, should be regarded as significant, and a veterinarian's advice should be sought.

*Left:* Grooming forms an important part of a cat's life. Its primary purpose is to keep the coat in order, but cats will also groom each other as a sign of friendship. The big cats, too, groom each other.

*Right:* With all his senses alert, a domestic tabby carefully checks his environment. He doesn't need to see the grass blade on the right; his sensitive whiskers have just told him it's there.

Cats' eyes are particularly well adapted for their naturally nocturnal life-style. Their ability to see in dim light is roughly 50 per cent more acute than that of a typical human; they cannot, contrary to popular belief, see in complete darkness. It is the advanced structure of the retinal cells that gives the cat its acute vision, while a reflective coating on the retina, not unlike a television screen, produces the familiar "cat's eye" effect and enhances night vision.

This extreme sensitivity to light would produce an opposite effect in bright daylight, where the cat would be frequently dazzled, if it could not contract the iris – the shutter in front of the lens – to a slit, thereby excluding surplus light.

### Sense of smell

Unlike some breeds of dog, the cat's sense of smell does not appear to operate well at long range, though it is very efficient when close-up. Cats habitually smell their food before tasting it to check whether it is to their liking, and, as many infuriated owners know, will sometimes reject it untasted if it is unfamiliar. Smell also plays a part when a cat is exploring an unfamiliar situation, or one which has been changed in some way, for example by the re-arrangement of furniture.

Smell is also a significant sense in the cat's sexual life. Here, the so-called Jacobson's organ, a sac of receptive cells in the roof of the mouth, gives rise to the flehmen reaction, a strange posture in which the cat lifts its head and opens it mouth, breathing in and flicking the smell back with its tongue. The plant catnip or catmint (*Nepeta cataria*) also arouses this response in about half the cat population, followed by ecstatic rolling and treading.

Aided by their ability to turn their ear-flaps in any desired direction, like television "dish" antennae, cats' hearing is acute and highly accurate in range- and direction-finding. It is able to detect high-pitched sounds well out of the range of human hearing, and, significantly, many of the species it preys upon – mice, voles and birds, for example – emit sounds of the higher frequencies. The hearing seems, however, to be the sense in cats most vulnerable to ageing (as indeed it is, especially in regard to the higher frequencies, in humans), and the range of detectable frequencies begins to narrow from the age of three or four. Many older cats become completely deaf, with a consequent sharp decline in their hunting efficiency and their ability to protect themselves, for example against road traffic.

*Below:* Colorpoint in full bloom. But, as the scent shows, some other cat has been there first. The question is, whose territory is this, and who is most prepared to defend it?

*Right:* Vision of horror – or just a cat at sunset? The unearthly glow from the eyes of this evening wanderer is, in fact, only the reflection of external light from the *tapetum lucidum* in the eye.

One of the biggest surprises for first-time cat owners is the repertoire of sounds that a cat can produce. A contributor to the *American Journal of Psychology* has identified no less than 16 different sounds associated with particular meanings.

Few cats have such a wide vocabulary, and the most common sounds are: a purr of contentment, which may range from the slightest sigh to a full-throated rumble; a bird-like chirrup of welcome; a hiss, typically used if an owner tries to give a cat medicine; a squeak of pain; and the "feed me" miaow. Among themselves, cats have another vocabulary of snarls, wails, growls and hisses, as well as the distinctive and raucous language associated with mating.

The purring of its mother after she has given birth is the first sound a kitten hears, and the purr and the distress call are the first language it learns. House cats tend to be more vocal, and have a greater range of vocabulary, than those living in less close contact with people, and, as with children, language development comes with language experience: the more you talk to your cat, the more it will "talk" to you. A stray brought into a new environment may, even if it has developed a language with a previous owner, take some time to respond to the new owner's conversation. But there are some cats, of course, which are disdainful of gossip and will vocalize only to express their own needs.

There is disagreement among biologists about the mechanism of the purr. Some place its source in the so-called "false vocal cords", two membranes behind the true vocal cords, and certainly, when a cat is in full purr the vibrations can be felt most strongly with a finger laid across the throat. Other scientists trace the sound to resonances in the skull.

## Gestures

The voice is only one means of communication. Cats also use their noses, facial expressions, paws, tails and indeed their whole bodies. Friendly cats greet each other by touching noses and mutual sniffing. An angry cat puts its ears back and its whiskers forward, and a frightened one flattens both ears and whiskers. Such permutations of the facial features are used to express the whole range of emotions from extreme anger to blissful pleasure.

The tail is raised high in greeting, whether to humans or to friendly cats, but a waving tail is a gesture of arousal, seen both in anger and when close to the prey in hunting. As for general body language, the habit of brushing against the owner's legs is a scent-marking exercise as well as a greeting, and some cats will extend this by licking the owner's legs or feet. Another mark of affection shown in some cases is to pat the owner's leg or even face with a paw, claws sheathed.

From the very considerable range of activity indicated here each cat will draw its own selection. Close contact, time and patience will enable many owners to extend and deepen their communication with their cat, and learn what signals to look for and to give.

*Above:* Body language. Tail up and tip-tilted, this sociable tabby has come to greet its owner at the door.

Cats are skilled at recognizing the sound of their owners' footsteps or voices.

*Above:* A cat with its fur fluffed out looks bigger and more frightening than it really is. This scared white kitten is acting big in answer to a threat from behind those bars.

*Right:* What is it trying to say? This young kitten has still got everything to learn – including the business of cat (and chicken) language.

Even in the house, a cat can often be seen demonstrating the skills that mark it out as a supreme hunter. Watch it negotiate the objects on a window-ledge as it makes for a place in the sun, or see it chasing, toying with and finally killing a ball of rolled-up paper.

The delicate tread and the precise appreciation of space are items of hunting equipment as vital as the cat's speed of movement and sharp claws. The retractable claws come out not only for the kill, but also when climbing. Their sharpness is essential to the feline way of life, and this is why facilities should always be provided, even for housebound cats, for them to be sharpened. Otherwise, a cat will choose its own scratching-post, which could well be your most priceless piece of furniture.

## Going for speed

The cat walks on tiptoe (the biologist's description is digitigrade) and this makes for speed since, in a fast sprint, the foot need have only minimal contact with the ground. The cat's flexible spine enables it to stretch and so lengthen the stride when running. The one quality that cats lack is endurance of physical effort – the hunt itself is broken down into a series of short chases – and this is why, for example, that they will usually catch only very young, very old or sick rabbits; but the cat makes up for this with perseverance and a long attention span.

Most predators will lose interest if the chase is too protracted, and turn away in search of another prey; but having identified their potential victims, most cats are prepared to watch and wait for their moment with incredible concentration. Compared with the blundering, well-meaning but hopeless hunting tactics of many dogs, the cat's economy of effort, combined with its determination, is admirable.

## Balancing act

Of immense value, both in hunting and in going about its ordinary everyday business, is the cat's ability to walk without difficulty on very narrow walkways such as roof ridges, tree branches, and narrow fences and walls. This is possible because of its rounded chest, the arrangement of its shoulder-blades (scapulae) at the sides, and the tail, used as a balancing-pole.

The cat's jumping and climbing abilities make the efforts of even the fittest and most athletic humans look puny – but then we have not been perfecting our techniques continuously throughout our evolution. Most cats enjoy a run up a tree for the sheer fun of it, and are expressing their hunting instinct, even if there is no prey in view.

Often, a cat will take an extended run, and then apparently simply keep on running when horizontal changes to vertical; in that split second, however, the claws will have been unsheathed, for they are the prime climbing tools. It will then find a suitable spot to rest while considering any more intricate work among dense branches or foliage. Cats that get stuck up trees have, more often than not, either been chased there or

*Above:* With a leap, a scrabble and a series of clawing jerks, this dedicated climber heads for the heights. Coming down is more difficult, but the nearby fence will probably help.

have ventured too far in the unthinking pursuit of a quarry. When they are out climbing for fun, most cats have a reasonable sense of how far they dare go.

In jumping, the cat will, unless the jump is familiar or the thrill of the chase too much to bear, usually "sight" the distance carefully, moving its head up and down to work out the perspective. This is critical, especially if it is jumping on to a narrow ledge where there is no room for error in landing. For many owners, one of the joys of cat-watching is the contrast in movement between the crouch-and-spring of a really fine jump and the precision of landing.

What goes up must come down, and in this cats are generally less elegant. The journey that, on the way up, was a beautifully smooth movement can, coming down, turn into an undignified scramble. If the only answer is for the cat to hurl itself into space and hope for the best, it will tend to fling itself away so as to make a less vertical and heavy landing. In such emergencies, and in the case of a straightforward fall, the flexible spine enables a cat to spiral its body so that it lands on its feet.

*Right:* An American brown Burmese patrolling its territory: it adopts a stolid, ready-for-anything prowl, but could leap into a sprint or a pounce at a moment's notice.

*Below:* Point work. An intent tabby demonstrates the cat's skill as a balancer: the legs on one side are walking along the very top of the fence, while the others are on another level altogether.

# Sex and reproduction

The sex life of the averagely healthy, un-neutered cat makes the most promiscuous human being look like a saint. Left to themselves, queens reach sexual maturity early – exceptionally, in some breeds, at three months, but more usually at six months. Toms mature slightly later, typically at nine months. The fertility cycle (oestrus) of a queen who does not find a mate is almost continuous. It is possible for a queen to have three litters a year. A roving tom in a territory which includes an adequate number of queens can spend something like three-quarters of the year in continuous pleasure. All this explains why the question of neutering or spaying is so important in the cat world.

## Looking for a mate

The symptoms shown by a queen entering the fertility cycle are unmistakable. There is, first, the "call" – a howl that varies between different breeds, and between individual cats, but which is most pronounced in the Siamese, whose queens are generally acknowledged to be the nymphomaniacs of catdom. It is said that the call of a Siamese queen can be heard across open country up to six miles away.

The queen will also show a marked increase in affectionate gestures, rubbing against people she knows,

*Above:* A feline courtship in progress. Although she is shut in, the smell (and the call) of the female have proclaimed to all the toms for miles around that she is in season and ready for mating.

*Left:* The moment of action. The black-and-white queen has been mounted by the tom of her choice, who is gripping her gently by the scruff of the neck. Penetration is over in a few seconds.

*Right:* If a mating is successful, results can be expected in about 62 days. The female kittens of this Siamese could themselves start to call when they are six months old.

rolling over in apparent pleasure, being much more vocal than usual, and often, when touched, adopting the crouch position which is standard for feline intercourse. Treading of the paws, increased urination, and spraying when outside are further signs.

This behavior will attract a following of toms, who will return the queen's calls. When she accepts a suitor – he may not nominate himself unless she agrees – they may mate several times in a single voluptuous session, and he may then be followed by another.

The copulation of cats never looks or sounds very much like pleasure, and indeed a virgin queen, not having a lot of fun herself, can give the tom a pretty rough time. When cats are deliberately mated, the advice is always to let the virgin tom have his first experience with a seasoned queen with her first litter behind her.

After a courtship which may last several hours, with much feinting and shadow-work, or may consist of only a few token passes, the tom immobilizes the queen by grabbing the nape of her neck, and she adopts the crouch position. Then he mounts her. It is all over in a few seconds, and the occasion is marked by a piercing cry from the queen, who tears herself away and turns on her partner. If he has any sense, he jumps clear to await his next opportunity.

An insensitive tom who has judged the wrong moment – or the wrong queen – to mount is liable to be attacked. However, in a protracted session, if only one tom is present, the queen will warm up and positively encourage further bouts. The scream of the queen when the tom withdraws is thought to be due to the presence of rasping spines at the tip of the tom's penis which may have a function in stimulating ovulation.

## Kittens with two fathers

A queen can, in fact, have kittens by two toms at the same time, if she has mated within the same fertility cycle. Normally, however, a successfully mated queen will stop calling, and so will attract no further attention from toms. The pregnancy may well not be evident for a month or more. The pregnancy lasts for about nine weeks – though the parameters allow for one week each side of this – and four is the typical number of kittens in a litter. A final note of warning: unlike human mothers, the queen is able to ovulate while she is still feeding her young. Although most will be busy enough supporting and teaching their kittens, some negligent mothers may, before the weaning period, decide to go in search of, or may be sought out for, fresh adventures. The result can be a cat with too many kittens.

Considering their life expectancy of somewhere between 12 and 16 years – and some live well into their twenties – kittens develop remarkably quickly. At birth, they weigh between 3.5-5.5 oz (100-155 g), and from then on they almost double their weight each week. By two weeks their milk teeth can be seen, followed by the adult teeth at four to six months. Males and females are fully grown at one year. So a kitten can expect to spend over 90 per cent of its life as an adult, compared with about 75 per cent for humans and about 80 per cent for dogs. In a fast-breeding species, the viability of the young at an early age is, of course, essential to survival.

### Early days

Given an attentive mother – and most queens are – and an interested owner and family, the young kitten's horizons and experiences expand very fast. It will spend the first week, when its eyes are still closed, asleep when it is not being fed. In the second week the eyes open, and by the third the kitten will be beginning to explore and play with its mother and the other kittens in the litter.

At this stage, differences in personality can be discerned by its willingness or reluctance to play adventurously, its attitude to the other kittens, and so on. From then on, play skills develop rapidly, and by the fifth and sixth weeks the specific hunting skills can be seen to develop. The kittens should be left with their mother until they are about three months old, for they have to be taught hunting "on the job". She will also give them a certain amount of discipline – most queens are quite firm mothers – as well as teaching them to be wary of possible dangers in their environment and housebreaking them.

*Above left:* A day-old black kitten cries out for the warmth, food and comfort of its mother.

*Above right:* Four days old and feeding well. The "kneading" reaction stimulates milk flow.

### Obesity

Fully-grown males tend to weigh in between 8-12 lb (3.6-5.4 kg) – towards the top of the range if neutered – and queens 5-7 lb (2.2-3.1 kg). Many cats, of course, exceed these top limits, though few as drastically as the 43 lb (19.5 kg) nine-year-old tom reported a few years ago in Connecticut. Since they exercise themselves, and tend to eat only until their hunger is satisfied, cats do not often have obesity problems.

At five or six months, kittens pass out of the extremely playful, typically "kittenish" phase into more sober adolescence. For the next six years or so, cats are in the prime of their lives. Neutering seems to make for longevity, but this may be due less to the operation itself than to the fact that neutered cats are less likely to roam and so are less vulnerable to accidents. Middle age sets in at about eight years. Toms gradually become jowly, and both toms and queens may gray around the mouth. Although queens may continue to mate until about twelve, the quality of their litters begins to drop steadily after about eight. Toms, however, will continue to sire kittens well into their teens if they get the chance, though declining agility and the rival attractions of younger toms may restrict their activities.

*Right:* With eyes now open and whiskers a-twitch, these little tabbies are ready to start making sense of their surroundings.

# 3 CATS IN THE HOME

If you take a cat into your home – or, for that matter, if a stray invites itself in, and you accept it – you are offering it a place in your family. This is not merely a sentimental thought, but a fact of cat psychology. You and your children will be regarded by the cat as substitutes for its own family unit, and this is the reason why cats allowed outdoors will sometimes bring back from their hunting expeditions an occasional bird or mouse corpse to add to the family larder.

Cats vary enormously, of course, in their sociability, their degree of vocalization, and their character. But even a hard-living stray brought into a family can, with care and attention, be taught to respond to affection. Few cats are going to resist the charms of a regular supply of palatable food without all the trouble of hunting for it – and what cat can hunt for delicious tidbits like sardines or tuna? If you make life pleasant for it, any cat will eventually repay you with such gestures of thanks as rubbing its muzzle against you, or washing your feet, or simply climbing on to your lap.

As far as more positive activity goes, there is no doubt that it is easier to bring up a kitten to be playful and vocal, and to respond to everyone in the family, than to train an older cat that has had limited domestic experience. However, this can be done – and remember that your newly-found stray is likely to be someone else's lost pet, and it may be a matter of going through the repertoire of different approaches (using the suggestions for play on pages 27 and 57, for example) until you trigger off a response from the stray's domestic past.

In any family, with cats as with children, there have to be rules. If you approach the bringing up of a cat in the same way as the bringing up of children, combining firmness with love, you will find your newly-acquired cat both pleasurable and rewarding.

*Left:* A place in the family (its human members are not on show). If care is taken with the introductions, cats and dogs can often learn to accept each other quite happily.

If you thought that the question of whether to have a cat was a simple yes-and-no-matter, you were wrong. Let's consider some of the variables. Do you want a mature cat or a kitten? Have you got the money to pay for a pedigree Persian, say, or will you be happy with a companionable mongrel? Are you prepared to give a home to a lost cat or a stray? Do you want a tom or a queen?

Even before you consider these questions, there are some other things to think about. Cats are good at looking after themselves, but they inevitably take up some time. They have to be fed, groomed, provided with a litter tray, let in, let out – and, most important, time has to be set aside to play with and cuddle them. If you are away from home for long periods every day, you will need to think about installing a cat-door.

## Who benefits most?

An important consideration is the age and health of the person who will be the cat's nominal owner. Remember that a few people, notably asthmatics and sufferers from eczema, must rule out cat ownership, and even the prolonged presence of a cat, because they are allergic. A few young children are actually frightened of cats and never take to them, usually because of some experience in early babyhood. However, there is convincing medical evidence that pets in general – and we can extend this to cats in particular because of their relative self-sufficiency – are a positive benefit to some elderly people as well as to the depressed, bereaved and lonely – though the basic reason for having cats must remain that the owner loves them.

Your choice will also depend on where you live. It would be a waste of money, to say nothing of good breeding, to buy a Himalayan if you live on a farm and expect it to share the rough and tumble of the farmyard. It would, of course, probably be ready to join in with gusto, but grooming problems would be enormous. Your apartment may, on the other hand, be small enough for you to have to consider the ultimate adult size, and the degree of activity, of your choice; some breeds are renowned for being super-active.

## Show cats

Having pondered all this, you may be ready to start being selective. If, like seven per cent of Americans, you favor a pedigree cat and hope one day to breed and possibly show, you have little choice but to go for a kitten. In your case, your most important choice, before you get down to considering individual breeds, is between short- and long-hairs; the latter require a considerable amount of regular and devoted grooming. Your best next step is to go to the largest cat show you can reach, and compare breeds.

You will find that owners of show cats will, in general, be happy to discuss breed characteristics with you. Advertisements in the show program will give you

*Left:* Well – which? All these silver tabby kittens are equally enchanting, so choice is difficult. There is only one answer: stay still and see which one decides to choose you.

*Right:* Two bouquets. The bright coloring of this pretty litter and their mother rivals that of the flowers beside them.

some names and addresses of likely breeders. Other sources of names are local newspapers and, of course, word of mouth. Personal recommendation is usually the best testimonial.

Unless you intend to breed, the choice between male and female is almost irrelevant except for personal taste. Whichever sex you choose, you will probably want to have the cat neutered.

It is a kindly thought to give a home to a stray, and in fact a surprisingly large proportion of owners acquire their cats that way, often because the cats choose them rather than the other way round. Act with caution, though, and do not accept a stray simply because you feel sorry for it.

If you do take to it and it seems to take to you, at the first opportunity have it inspected by a veterinarian, who will be able to tell you its approximate age, its condition, and if it has any defects. The same applies to any cat or kitten that you may be offered as a gift or by a well-meaning neighbor.

Cats' homes usually have both adults and kittens available, and it is especially important when choosing from one of these institutions to keep a clear and rational head – cats in cages can look both pathetic and winsome. Having made all these reservations, however, it has to be said that very many people have had long-lasting, loving, and entirely satisfactory relationships with strays, lost cats or cat orphans. One last thought, though: never have a cat "wished on you" if you are not really enthusiastic.

## Adapting to the home

Although the cat's natural lifestyle is nocturnal, it adapts easily enough to fit in with humans. The only exceptions may be cats that you take on as adults and that have lived nocturnally under their previous ownership, but even here it is worth while, once the newcomer has settled in with you, trying the "night in" routine.

Some old cats are even less ready than old dogs to learn new tricks, however, and if it is clear that you are disturbing your cat's life too profoundly, you might as well give in. Such special cases apart, there seems little point, since most cats adapt so readily, in exposing them to the hazards of the traditional "cat out" routine: bad weather, sudden traffic in the still of the night, possible theft, and, above all, the temptation to roam arising from eight or more hours away from human attention.

### Necessary routines

Like most pets, and like many human beings, cats obtain reassurance from the fact that today is like yesterday, and tomorrow will be like today. They will set up their own routines, and will play their part if you play yours. Details will depend as much on your lifestyle as on theirs, but here is a description of a typical cat's day. Compare it with that of your own.

*Above:* Fright or fascination? A kitten exploring every corner of its new garden.

*Below:* The youngest animal on the farm makes friends with the farmer's sheepdog.

● It rises at first light and uses its litter tray, and then fills in the time until its owner is up by patting a toy mouse and limbering up for the real hunting which (it hopes) the new day will bring.

● It will greet its owner with a chirp and a rub, and eat its morning meal, perhaps leaving some to be finished later. A quick wash will be followed by stepping out for an hour or so.

● Coming in, it will sleep for several hours – some cats are capable of sleeping for 18 hours out of the 24 without feeling they are missing out on anything – before making another foray in, say, the late afternoon.

● It will then return when called for its second meal, and leaving this until after the last-light hunting session is a useful inducement.

● After another wash, probably a more extended affair this time, it will be ready to join the family for the evening's entertainment.

This is only a day in the life of a *typical* cat, remember; yours may work quite differently. There will also be seasonal differences; short days and cold weather make a cat less adventurous, whereas, on a balmy summer's night, you may well have difficulty in persuading your cat to come in.

## Undivided attention

Most people find evening the time when they can best spare attention for their pets. As with children, you should try to build into your day some time when you can give your cat undivided and undisturbed attention. It may enjoy a game with a piece of string or a ball of wool, or it may simply want to climb on a friendly lap and be stroked; though not all cats are lap-cats, and some are happier just to sit with the family in a cosy spot and quietly enjoy their company.

If your cat is new, this is the time when you will get to know it, and it you. You will learn which particular caresses it enjoys, and which make it spit. It will also, during these quiet, domestic times, decide upon its various places for sitting and dozing. You may find some of these odd. Quite probably, the answer will lie in the position of central heating pipes or ducts under the floor. But for many cat-owners, and probably for many cats, these quiet moments of companionship are the highspots of their relationship.

*Below:* More explorations. This time, the newcomer is older than the established resident. Mature cats can make beautiful pets, if they are given extra encouragement to settle down.

47

Just by looking at these kittens, you are probably quite prepared to name your first choice, but beware: appearance alone is not a good criterion. Choosing a kitten is something you should do when you have plenty of time to spend with the litter, watching and playing. If you are a first-time owner, you are looking for specific qualities; a breeder making a choice from the same litter would have other considerations. These words are addressed to first-time buyers.

You want a kitten that will be sturdy, companionable, and pleasant to live with. In all this, personality is the only reliable guide. You will not be able to reform a thug kitten, or bring out a shrinking one. Too many human relationships have unhappily foundered on such delusions, and animals are no different in this respect.

## The right personality

Watch the kittens at play and then, quietly and without fuss, join them. (Excuse yourself and leave any seller who does not allow you to do this.) Initially, wait for them, or one of them, to come to you. Very likely, the first to come will be your ultimate choice, but watch all of them with care. Confidence is one thing; "pushiness" is another, and if you are looking for a pet cat you want one which can respect and obey rules, not one that is going to rule you.

Look out particularly for the neurotic, the bully, and the born loser, and reject them. The kitten that is nervous and shy, running away to hide, is going to be hard work to bring on as a self-sufficient cat. The plus signs are alertness, agility and bounce, and a willingness on the kitten's part to take an investigative interest in you. This may start with a cautious sniff, or a delicate whiskering, and extend to climbing on to your knee or lap and purring.

## Health and fitness

So much for the kitten's personality. Now for the question of health. Unless you are an experienced cat-owner, you will not be qualified to look for much more than obvious signs of weakness or sickness such as dull or

*Above:* Curiosity is always a plus sign. But what about vanity? In fact, cats and kittens are often fascinated by mirrors – and by whatever is (or isn't) behind these puzzling things.

gummy eyes. The best plan, when you have made your choice, is to arrange to purchase it subject to a veterinary examination. Finally, assuming that this is in order, you will need the kitten's "papers" – its vaccination certificate and, if it is a pedigree kitten and you have any thoughts of breeding or showing at some time in the future, its pedigree certificate and registration documents.

One word of warning: do not give in to appeals to take the children with you when choosing a kitten. For one thing, they will go for the most appealing, which may not necessarily be the best choice, and this will only mean heartbreak. Also, children get wildly excited on such occasions and will excite or frighten the kittens. Remember that you are choosing a pet which may be your companion for 15 years or more: take as much thought over it as you would over choosing a spouse!

*Left:* As like as peas in a pod, as the saying is. This big litter of Somali kittens has lined up in an ideal way for a buyer – but it makes sense to watch them all in action for a while first.

*Right:* Copycats. The kitten's first and most important teacher is always its mother; a lot can be learned about its talents and personality by watching the mother in action as well.

Before you bring your new acquisition home, whether it is a cat or a kitten, there is a certain amount of preparatory work to be done and some essential items of equipment need to be bought.

The first thing you must decide is where the cat is going to have its base – that is, its bed and, unless you have a cat door, its litter tray. (You will need at least a temporary tray in any case.) These should be in the same room but, for obvious reasons, not too close to each other. The best base is one where the cat can have peace when it wants it, where it will not be disturbed by children or the general activities of the household. Cats like to be discreet at the toilet.

## Beds and litter trays
There is really no need, unless you are fussy about appearances, to go to the expense of a specially-made cat bed (and it will not help your new relationship if, having done so, you find that the cat prefers to sleep under the couch or in an old chair, which is quite likely). A cardboard box lined with a piece of old blanket is quite adequate. Purpose-made litter trays can be bought from pet stores, but any container which is big enough and can be sterilized is suitable. Commercially made cat litter, though expensive, is easiest to deal with and contains a deodorant, but peat moss, sand or soil are all acceptable to the cat.

The other item that you will need immediately – indeed, to collect your new pet in – is a cat basket or other container. There will be a continuing need for this when you take the cat to the veterinarian and if you intend to travel with it to any extent. (Never be tempted to drive with a cat loose in the car – it's suicidal.) Any self-respecting cat will claw its way out of a cardboard container within minutes, and even if it doesn't the container will soon become grubby.

If you are going to spend a substantial amount on any item for the cat, a proper basket is a good investment. Various wire, wood, plastic or wicker types are available. Remember to allow for an adult-size cat. Newspaper makes a suitable lining material.

Treat a newly-arrived kitten as you would a baby coming home for the first time and you won't go far wrong. Remember that this will be its first really big experience since birth. It may be frightened or overexcited, or both in turns.

*Left:* The very first thing your new cat will need, after it settles down, is something to eat. And the second thing is something to eat it from. A flat dish is better than a bowl for food, and its water bowl should also be as shallow as possible.

*Right:* From behind the safety of glass, this ginger pet watches the world go by below. The windows frequented by high-living cats should always be kept shut, or protected by wire screens.

## New surroundings

Keep all doors and windows closed, securely guard any open fires completely, and firmly block any unused chimneys. The kitten's first reaction will almost certainly be to try to escape. Avoid sudden noises and, if you have children, restrain them from picking up the new arrival. If you explain that it must be given time to settle in and that the children can "watch but not touch", most will see the sense of this. Babies, though, are best kept out of the way.

The kitten, and even an adult cat for that matter, is likely to hide for a time while it assesses the sounds and smells of its new environment. Have food and water at hand, but do not be in too much of a hurry to offer it. (It should be in the place that you have decided on as the permanent feeding-station.) Eventually, the kitten will emerge from its hiding-place and, while everyone keeps very still and quiet, begin to explore.

You may need to show it its litter tray, which it may want to use after all the excitement, and its bed. Make sure, if you are using a cardboard box, that the kitten can get in and out easily. With luck, your new pet will then have a short grooming session and then settle down for a sleep.

Particular care is needed if there are other cats or dogs in the house. Initially, they are best out of the way, with the new cat confined to one room. (This may call for some advance planning.) Despite closed doors, each will soon become aware of the other's scent, and in any case the older resident will know that there is something unusual going on. Let the newcomer be thoroughly settled before you do the introductions. Even if these go well, don't leave resident and newcomer alone together for a day or so, until you are sure how they have taken to each other. It is probably best to feed them separately, at least for the first few days, and it is wise as well as courteous to observe seniority and always feed and pay attention to the older resident before the newcomer.

In addition to a bed, litter tray and basket mentioned previously, there are a number of other basic requirements. Cats have three principal needs: food, sleep and shelter. Food first, then.

If you have bought a kitten from a breeder, you will have been given a diet sheet for you to follow for the first weeks. (If a diet sheet is not offered, ask for one.) If you are taking over an adult cat from a known previous owner, find out what its favorite foods, commercial brands and tidbits are, and whether it likes milk or cream (not all cats do, despite the folk tales). Almost all cats are very choosy about their food, and some maintain complete loyalty to one particular flavor of one particular brand of canned or dried food.

When planning any change in an adult cat's regimen, whether in feeding times or the number of feeds or types of food, do so gradually, watching carefully to check any constipation or diarrhea. It is best to delay any such changes for the first couple of weeks. Food and water bowls may be made of any material that can be easily cleaned and sterilized.

*Left:* Checking his weight gain. This method works well with a kitten but, to weigh an adult cat, get on the bathroom scales, pick the cat up – and notice the difference between the two weights.

*Below:* The pushy red tabby is probably getting more than his fair share of milk. It's best to give each kitten in a group its own separate bowls, both for food and drink, to ensure fair shares.

## Claw sharpening

Something that any cat needs to do is to sharpen its claws. It is possible, if you have a garden with trees, that it will do this outside, but most likely – and certainly in the case of a young kitten – you will need to provide indoor facilities if you value your furniture and carpets.

Scratching posts and pads can be bought from pet stores, or you can make serviceable ones by tacking coconut matting or carpet (but not carpet of a type used in your own home – use a leftover piece from someone else) to a log or a block of wood. If you are ambitious, you can provide your pet with a real adventure playground made out of rustic lengths of wood, and a kitten in particular will enjoy this – but take care to make it stable and, of course, to conceal all nails or drive them well in.

You will need a small set of grooming tools: a small hairbrush of the handled, semi-circular type with fairly soft bristles, a comb with two different sets of teeth, and some absorbent cotton are adequate to start with.

It is worth noting here that, just as the newly-arrived cat has to establish its routines in your home, so do you have to establish yours in relation to your new responsibility. Longhairs need to be groomed each day, though for shorthairs, unless they are molting, once a week is enough. The grooming session should also include a check over teeth, eyes and coat.

Grooming, as well as the other duties you have committed yourself to, should be part of a set routine which also includes providing fresh water (several times a day, especially in summer), feeding, cleaning the dirt tray (again, possibly more than once, and certainly last thing at night), and, of course, playtime.

More detailed information on the day-by-day care of the cat is given in Chapter 7.

*Below:* An owner who's beginning as she means to go on. All longhairs need to be groomed daily, and, to make it a pleasure for everyone involved, they should get used to it young.

Veterinary opinion is virtually unanimous in supporting the neutering or spaying of cats from which you do
not intend to breed. This helps reduce the number of
unwanted kittens, many of which are turned out of the
home to become strays, and makes the cat-owner's life
much easier.

Queens in season are noisy and may spray in the
house; entire (uncastrated) toms will certainly spray,
and their urine is particularly smelly. Neutered cats are
generally more affectionate and better-tempered, and
are not as vulnerable as un-neutered ones to the hazards
of roaming, or to physical damage as a result of fights.
Without placing unacceptable restrictions on its movements, it is practically impossible to prevent an entire
tom from finding a series of mates or a queen in season
being mounted by a succession of toms. Note that
neutering does not prevent the cat-owner, if he or she
wishes, from enjoying the pleasures of showing.

Reflecting the general belief of cat-lovers that neutering is advisable except in cats specifically kept for breeding, there are special classes for neutered cats at all
shows, with "premier" rather than "championship"
titles being awarded to the winners.

Some owners believe that it is fair to a queen to give
her one opportunity to bear and rear kittens before
spaying her. This is fine, provided that you have the
time to take care of her during pregnancy, and have clear
plans for the destinations of the kittens afterwards.
Otherwise, female kittens are spayed from about six
months (though opinion varies on the minimum suitable age, and you will want to take your veterinarian's
advice) or at any time after that up to about six years.

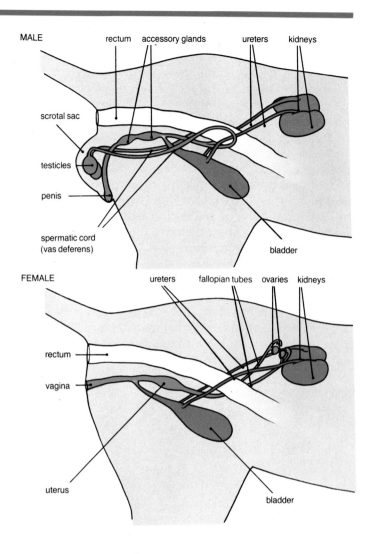

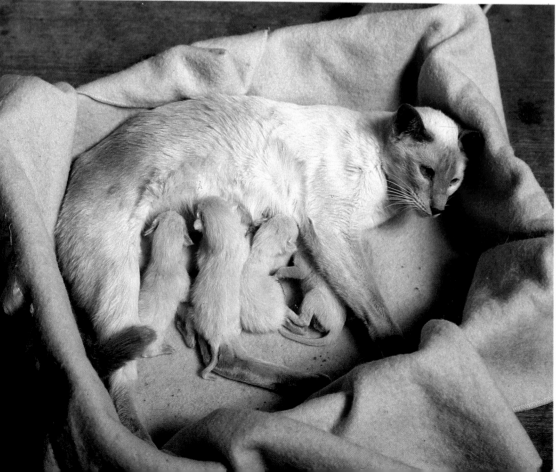

*Above:* Shown in blue are the
reproductive organs of the male
(upper diagram) and female cat.
The organs shown in red are the
kidneys and bladder. Neutering –
or castrating – a tom consists of
removing the testicles inside the
furry scrotum. Spaying a female is
a more complicated operation,
consisting of removing the ovaries
(shown close to the kidneys) and
the uterus.

*Left:* The planned family of a
pedigree pet will grow up as
pedigree-bearers themselves.
But, where breeding is not
intended, neutering pet cats works
in the favor of both owner and cat.

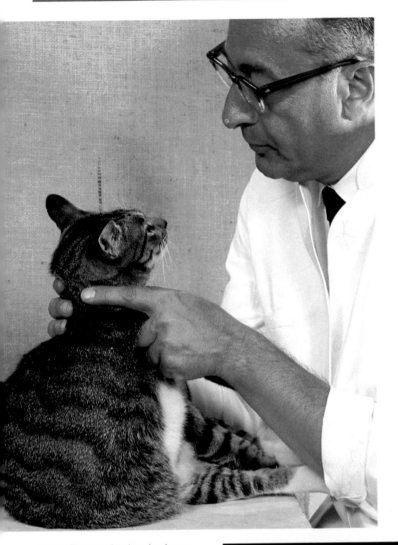

## Surgery

The operation, which is performed under general anesthetic, removes the ovaries, fallopian tubes and uterus. The area in which the incision is made – in the abdomen or on the flank – is shaved for the operation, but the hair quickly grows again and the cat is effectively unmarked except in some Siamese and Himalayans, where the new hair comes up darker, and even then this is often a temporary fault which is corrected during the next molt.

The veterinarian will ask you not to give your cat food or water for a number of hours before the operation, and may keep it in overnight to check recovery from the anesthetic. No special after-care is needed, except for trying to discourage nibbling at the stitches and for keeping the cat quiet and indoors for two or three days.

## Recovery

The operation on males is simpler, takes only a few minutes, and again is performed from about six months onwards, under anesthetic. Recovery is rather quicker – usually within 24 hours – than with the female.

Most of the myths you might have heard about neutering and spaying are just that: *myths*. It is true that neutered males and even spayed females do tend to put on weight – but all this means is that you have to take a little more care in the amounts you feed. The extra weight, in any case, evidently does them no harm, for it is a statistical fact that neutered cats live longer than un-neutered. Nor is it true that neutering makes a male cat lazy and less inclined to hunt, as many owners of a neutered champion mouse hunter will agree.

*Above:* The veterinarian checks up on a patient's general state of health. Cats should not be neutered when they are too young to take the operation.

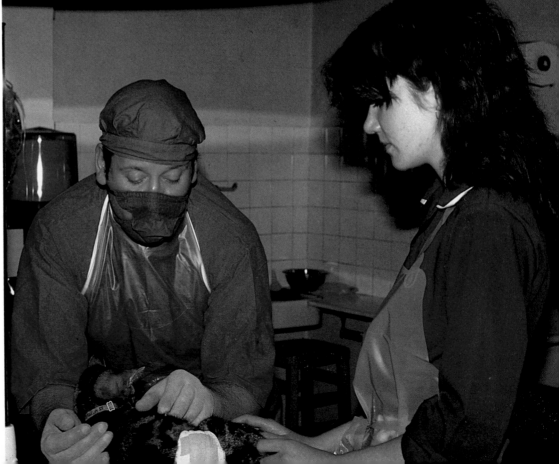

*Right:* In the operating theater. Both castrating and spaying operations are carried out under general anaesthetic. The patient usually goes home within a few hours or the next day.

Before you even start to think about choosing a particular cat, it is important to consider what kind of lifestyle it is going to have. Far too many kittens are brought into homes without sufficient forethought, only to be turned out when they are found to be "too much trouble" for one reason or another. Face any possible problems beforehand, and plan ahead for them.

In the United States (in contrast to Europe) majority opinion among experts seems to favor confining a cat indoors, especially in cities. (Europeans would tend to say that, pedigree and breeding cats apart, the indoor life may be a regrettable necessity but should be avoided if possible.)

*Above:* Indoor playthings need not be expensive. A paper bag will provide lots of fun – until it falls to pieces. But cats must never be allowed to play with plastic bags. Suffocation is a real danger.

*Left:* A seal point Siamese tom sizes up his jump carefully before leaping.

## Protection *v* freedom

As with young children, there is a conflict here between giving cats protection and allowing them freedom. The balance seems to come down in favor of protection where young kittens, breeding and pedigree cats are concerned, and possibly, in cities, for all cats. At the same time, there is a case for letting cats enjoy the outdoor life during the day where this is possible. What is certain is that if you take on a mature cat you should let it continue its life in the style to which it is accustomed.

It is perfectly possible, however, given ingenuity on the part of the owner, to provide a relatively exciting environment for a cat even within an apartment, at little or no cost. A paper bag (but *never* any kind of plastic one) makes an exciting toy for a kitten, though it will not last long. A cardboard box with a suitably-sized hole cut in it will provide great enjoyment, as will a cardboard tube, open at both ends, large enough for the cat to go through; but check for protruding pins or staples. A sheet of corrugated cardboard, rolled into a tube and secured with sticky tape, is ideal, though it may be short-lived since some cats have a passion for tearing up corrugated cardboard, puppy-style. If you are really keen to spend money, pet stores have commercially-made versions of all these items, even down to cardboard boxes labelled, for the cat's information, "cat toy".

*Below:* A young owner finds that walking a cat on a lead is easier said than done. But it will get the idea in the end – perhaps.

## Forbidden areas

You must decide whether you are going to allow your cat the run of the house or confine it to certain areas. Initially, any restriction will involve the punctilious shutting of doors, but many cats will come to respect their owner's wishes if they are turned out of forbidden areas often enough, especially if care is taken to provide (and point out) an attractive alternative.

In areas where the cat is allowed, you will need to check that house-plants are out of reach (some are poisonous, and all react badly if their pots are used as litter-trays), along with any valuable or precious knick-knacks. The kitchen is a potentially dangerous place for cats and is best put out of bounds, if possible. Open fireplaces, even when the fire is not alight, should be securely guarded. Children's bedrooms or dens may contain such things as small plastic toys which could be dangerous if swallowed.

If you allow your cat out, there are a few obvious hazards to be avoided in the garden or yard. All water should be covered, and swimming-pools should have steps out. Any weedkillers or pesticides should be kept shut in a cupboard, and bait for rats or slugs must be sited so that it is impossible for the cat to get at it. No broken glass, empty plastic bags or other dangerous garbage should be left lying about. If you have a woodpile, make sure it is stable, since it is likely to attract rats or mice and, in turn, a hunting cat.

For further advice on the indoor management of cats, see pages 150-5 and 170-5.

*Left:* Staking its claim. Cats have
scent glands under their chins; by
"chinning" strategic parts of their
territories, they demonstrate their
presence and warn intruders off.

Showing as we know it is barely a century old, but the value of the cat as a controller of vermin has been acknowledged for at least 4000 years – and indeed, for most of that time, this has been the basis of the cat's relationship with man.

As can be observed in any kitten from the age of about four weeks, cats react instinctively to a twitching piece of string, and it is this reaction that it brings into play when it is hunting a mouse or a rat. The instinct can be maintained and reinforced by training from kittenhood, using string, but the best training for a hunting cat is done by the mother; so, when she is ready, let her take the kittens out and train them "on the job".

Toms have a good reputation as ratters, but unless you have a very large property you would probably be better off with a less far-ranging neuter or a queen. The tom may well catch more rats, but a higher proportion of them will be on someone else's land.

## Meals well earned

It is no good expecting a cat that you have acquired specifically to keep down vermin to double as a fully domesticated pet as well. For one thing, it will spend more time outdoors, and may well prefer to live outside. It will tend to follow the nocturnal lifestyle of the wild cat. A queen may go semi-feral, using the house as an occasional feeding-station and perhaps coming inside temporarily for warmth in cold, wet weather.

There is, by the way, no basis for the country belief that if you want a good ratter you should keep it hungry. Cats will kill rats and mice whether they are hungry or not, though they may eat enough not to need their next meal. If you want your champion ratter to stay on your premises, it is good sense to make it worthwhile by providing regular meals.

## Cats as killers

Bear in mind that a cat will kill not only mice and rats, but also a variety of other small animals. Some will be killed for sport, and may be brought back to the house as trophies or presents. This is a good sign, it shows that the cat knows what its business is, and wants your approval. If you value its hunting skills, the delivery of a corpse should bring praise and a tidbit as a reward. Remember, by the way, that a cat which spends a good deal of its time hunting will become trigger-happy, with possibly disastrous effects on the local bird life. If you encourage birds into your garden or yard by putting out food and water, make sure that this is in a position inaccessible to cats, on a bird-table well out of cat-reach.

Many people recoil with horror when they observe what they see as a cat's cruel, taunting behavior with captured prey. What looks like deliberate playing with a victim, however, more often illustrates the cat's instinctive hunting technique. It must be remembered that an adult rat, or even a large young one, is a formidable adversary for a cat – and indeed, cats trying to bite off more than they can chew sometimes come off worse or, at least, have to beat a dignified retreat from the confrontation. The key to success is for the cat to immobilize the rat as quickly as possible before moving in for the kill, and this is the inbuilt behavior that can be seen in what, to the unknowledgeable eye, is apparently play.

Another aspect of this instinct is seen when the cat "plays cat-and-mouse". This may happen when the cat thinks it has immobilized its victim and lifts its paw to check, only to allow the victim to sprint away. Alternatively, there are some cats so lacking in hunting skills that they literally allow their victims to slip through their paws, so that what looks like a horribly teasing game is often merely incompetence.

*Right:* A farmyard is a perfect hunting-ground – but the territory may be disputed. A big hen like this one is quite capable of putting a cat to flight, especially if she is defending her chicks.

*Left:* Both natural hunters, and both ready to go. But the cat will get off to a quicker start than its canine colleague. Cats often pick high places from which to spot likely prey to pounce on.

If a cat is going to share your home and your life, and both it and you are going to enjoy the experience, you both have to reach agreement on the kind of behavior you expect from each other. The cat expects you to feed, play and provide it with shelter, warmth and somewhere to sleep. You can reasonably expect of your cat that it will learn a few simple rules – for example, about not scratching the furniture or climbing up the drapes, and about coming when called – and that it will avoid behavior which you have indicated that you don't like.

## Survival skills

Mother cats teach their kittens the basic skills for survival, but they cannot be expected to act as the owner's assistant teachers in more complex matters. The owner's role as trainer begins as soon as a new kitten or cat is brought home, and it is as well to start by training it to come when called. Here, naming is important.

Your cat's name should be distinctive in vowel-sound and degree of sibilance from any other cats in the house, and preferably from any others in the neighborhood. (Remember that even a housebound cat may escape and need to be called in from outside.) Use the name frequently at mealtimes and when you are stroking and grooming, and encourage others in the household to do so to avoid the problem of the "one person" cat. Repeated calling of the name when the cat is in another room or outside can be trained as a "come here" signal, rewarded with a morsel. Another effective mealtime call is to beat a rhythm on a plate with a teaspoon.

## Disapproval

Another essential if you and your cat are going to live happily together is a signal indicating prohibition or disapproval. Never hit a cat – it is both dangerous and ineffective. But cats dislike sudden loud noises; so a sharp (not shouted) "No!", or a clap of the hands, or even a hiss, with perhaps a pointed finger for emphasis, is usually effective if accompanied by the firm but not rough removal of the cat from the prohibited place or

activity. Find out which sound works best, and then stick to it.

Spraying can be a problem with confined cats, and this is an argument for letting them spend at least some time outside if possible. Females spray to mark the boundaries of their territory, and if these are outside rather than inside the problem will disappear naturally.

Alternatively, there are various preventive measures – for example, picking up the cat and placing it firmly in its litter-tray. Oil of citronella, obtainable from a pharmacy, is a useful deterrent since almost all cats detest the smell. However, it is pungent, though not violently disagreeable, to humans too, so use only one or two drops dabbed on to the legs and frames of furniture, or on to painted wall or door surfaces, with a tissue. Wipe it off when the message has got across. It is also a deterrent against scratching.

### Using a cat door

If you have a cat door, you will need to teach your cat to use it. This can be done by tying a ball of paper to a length of string and feeding it through the door. Retreat to one side, leaving the paper and cat on the other, and gradually pull the ball through. Remember to do this from both sides to demonstrate that the door works both ways, and also that, as with any training you give a cat, you will have to repeat it several times and reinforce it in further sessions.

Any children in the house must also be trained – for example, in what tidbits they may feed, in resisting cats begging at table, and which areas of the house are out of bounds. Cats should not be allowed to sleep on beds, whether occupied or not, and they should be firmly banned from all kitchen working surfaces and from dining tables.

*Below:* Learning to live together. A wild game of tease-the-Spaniel is in progress – but the kittens know the rules. So does their big friend, who is not in fact much older. He may bite, but only gently.

One of the most important distinctions between the behavior of cats and dogs is that whereas, being pack animals, dogs tend to lead open and public lives, cats keep part of their lives to themselves or, at any rate, away from human gaze.

Many cat owners have been surprised by chance conversations with neighbors, sometimes years after they first owned a cat, to find how widespread and complex their cat's territory is. If you have a fairly large garden in a heavily cat-populated area, it makes an interesting activity for children to build a hideaway, and chart the comings and going of their own and neighboring cats during the course of a day.

### Territories

A cat's world can be seen as a series of concentric circles. In the center will be its main sleeping-place. From this radiates an area (typically, the parts of the house where it is permitted to go) which it knows well and in which it feels totally secure. Beyond this is its larger territory, which it will have established by scent-marking (spraying and rubbing) and which it will defend against rivals, at first by a staring-out match and then, if necessary, by fighting.

A new cat arriving in an area will have to carve out its territory against rival claims. In this, it will take its cue from its owner's movements. If you are seen pottering about in your garden or yard, giving every sign that you have "rights" there, this will be a signal that it is all right for the cat to follow suit.

The most vicious fights will be between a newcomer and a female cat with young, and with any ambitious visiting tom. Entire males have the widest territories, so wide indeed that they include almost any area where there is a female on heat.

### Hunting country

Ideally, a cat's territory will include a handful of pleasant places to snooze in the sun, to which it will go at appropriate times of the day, and a couple of high points from which it can survey – lazily or with acute interest, according to mood – the scene below. There will also be an area of hunting country.

Many cats will tour their territory as regularly and routinely as any police patrolman, as if keeping to a timetable which is probably dictated by the time that the sun reaches the various resting-places. They will often reach the starting-point and come back home by following exactly the same paths. Dogs may wander vaguely about in the garden, sniffing here and there. Cats are always more businesslike and purposeful.

Human beings may choose to take their daily jog or stroll at a quiet time when they are unlikely to meet anyone, or they may enjoy the companionship of their neighbors. So with cats. If they are left out at night they will often temporarily abandon their territories and seek the company of others on neutral ground. Others, especially in heavily cat-populated areas, "time-share" their territories and access routes with neighbors.

*Above:* A sense of territory starts young. The two kittens here are playing a war game well-known to human children.

*Below:* With ears flattened and teeth bared, this black-and-white prepares to defend his patch with all he's got.

*Right:* When a cat strops its claws, it is doing more than just cleaning them: it is also leaving a scent mark behind from the glands in its paws. Outdoor cats mark trees and fences; this indoor one is also marking an object in its territory.

*Below:* Waiting for the mail. Cats are choosy about the places where they like to sleep, both by day and by night, and the spots they choose may not always be the most convenient ones for the rest of the family.

POST

# 4 A GALAXY OF BREEDS

A dream of the future – or a throwback to last century, when cat breeders seemed to know secrets lost to us today? Until recently, that is how the shaded golden Persian would have been regarded in the international cat fancy: the exclusive and glamorous world of top cats, their owners and feline connoisseurs in general.

If, in the past, a shaded golden had turned up in a litter of silvery-colored cats, the owner would have shrugged with resignation and written the event off as one of nature's mistakes. In evolutionary terms, however, yesterday's mistake can be today's success story – and animal breeding is only an attempt by man to control evolution.

In cat circles as elsewhere, breeders sometimes set out to create an animal they have deliberately "designed"; just as often, however, they take advantage of the happy accidents that frequently occur on the feline production line. Among the results, either way, can be counted some of the world's most beautiful domestic animals.

But however different these magnificent pets may appear in coloring and shape, they retain one thing in common: they are all still cats and, in essentials, they function and behave just like the ordinary mouse catcher in the barn.

*Left:* Obviously high-born. These two young Persians both demonstrate one of the hallmarks of many pedigree cats: eyes that are not green or yellow, but a deep, glowing copper.

## Breeds

We have been breeding dogs – that is, exploiting their mating urges to create animals that conform to preconceived standards of appearance and behavior – for hundreds and even thousands of years. In contrast, we have been breeding cats for scarcely more than a century. It is a young science – or, as many would say, an art – and this is probably the reason why cats do not exhibit the enormous range of shapes, colors, sizes and capabilities demonstrated by dogs.

In terms of the cat's body structure, there are certainly one or two dramatic deviations from the norm, of which the Manx is the best-known and probably the oldest example. However – perhaps happily – attempts to engineer major changes in the feline shape have not been crowned with any great success; while larger-than-average cats do exist, breeders trying to go in the opposite direction and produce "toy" versions have found that the resulting kittens are sterile or have other defects.

In spite of this, however, there is still a respectable number of cat breeds in existence. It now stands at well over 100, for example, in Britain, where the system for classifying breeds reaches a peak of elaboration. (It was in the UK that methodical cat breeding was first pioneered.) In the US, the overall number is lower, but the number of sub-divisions within the various breeds is correspondingly high. And in both countries, new applicants for official breed status continue to appear.

## Definitions

The difference between US and UK practice over the question of breed classification highlights a matter of crucial importance to anyone involved in animal breeding. What exactly is a breed? One answer is that it is a distinctive group of domestic animals that always breeds true: a Persian mated to a Persian, for example, will produce Persian kittens.

While that is not the whole story (Manx matings, in particular, are fraught with surprises for the breeder), it is at least the bare bones of the plot; the problems come over the definition of the word "distinctive". There is no difficulty here, of course, with either Manx or Persian – but what about a blue Persian as opposed to a black one? Can breed definition rest simply on color alone, or should the animal's distinguishing marks display more fundamental differences from those of other breeds?

This question of color is only one of the thorny issues that face the various organizations responsible for breed definition and registration. (Both functions are extremely important in the cat fancy world, since they are the foundation upon which the whole structure of breeding and showing is built up. When pedigree kittens are born, a breeder registers them as members of their breed. A cat's pedigree is, in fact, its family tree, made up of the registered names and breed details of its parents, grandparents, and so on.)

## Registration organizations

The US has several registration organizations, of which the largest is the Cat Fanciers' Association. In Britain there is just one, the Governing Council of the Cat Fancy. Europe has its Fédération Internationale Féline, plus a number of national bodies. Canada has the Canadian Cat Association, while other countries with their own cat organizations include Australia and New Zealand.

Not surprisingly, this rich and admirable diversity is mirrored by a similar diversity of opinion as to which breed definitions count as acceptable in terms of color, shape, genetic make-up, and much else. And, within the English language alone, differences in breed and

color variety names have proliferated to an almost unmanageable extent.

## Shape and color

To sum up, it is fair to say that the US system – though it has its quirks – by and large defines breeds in terms of body shape (taken in its widest sense). The UK approach, followed in several other Old World countries, is to combine considerations of body shape with those of color. Taken together, these two factors of shape and color determine the appearance of all pedigree cats.

However, the permutations and combinations demonstrated in the different varieties may not, of course, always be the result of the breeder's program. Many breeds, of which the Maine Coon and the Siamese are only two, developed the essential distinguishing marks of their appearance by themselves, through natural selection. The breeder's job here is to produce improvements and refinements, and this is done through the lengthy and intricate process of mating cats that bear characteristics to be encouraged. Typically, though not always, the cats will be of the same breed.

At the same time, however, a breeder who is inspired to create, say, a Russian Blue longhair is certainly at liberty to try his or her luck, via a much more radical program of inter-breed crosses. Whether such a revolutionary scheme would produce worthwhile results is another matter; but cat breeders often relish a challenge, and it's an odds-on guess that someone, somewhere, has just such a program in mind.

The job is naturally made easier if the female cat starts things off by producing a kitten of unexpected but handsome appearance. Many of the most successful breeds and varieties have begun in this way, but their founding members have not always owed their novel qualities to a mismatch between a pedigree queen and an alley-cat. Often, the distinctive features involved are truly "accidental" in origin; they are the result of a minute error cropping up in the genetic code that is contained in the cells of all living creatures and that governs the creature's development.

The Rex breeds, with their curly fur, are examples of just such a genetic mutation, but, in fact, the vast majority of our pedigree cats (and many of our non-pedigree hearthside companions) are mutants as well. In its predomesticated state, the cat was a short-haired sandy tabby, and a long series of mutations has given its descendants such attractive new features as blue or red coloring, dark points, or long, flowing fur.

The following pages show how extensive these changes have been, and how the basic elements of coat length, body shape and color have been used to shape the pedigree breeds we know today.

*Above:* Breeding true to form. Like several other pedigree breeds, the Siamese developed its main distinguishing marks without human interference, as a completely natural process.

*Left:* A homely action for an extremely valuable cat. Red is one of the most difficult colors for breeders to get right, since tabby markings are always present. Here they are very faint.

*Right:* A new breed in the making? This pedigree tom owes his curly coat to one of the newer breeds, the Devon Rex. But, as his full cheeks show, he is in fact a hybrid, with domestic shorthair influence.

# Longhairs and shorthairs

The most obvious difference between the different types of pedigree cats is also one of the most fundamental: in some cats the fur is short, while in others it is long. There are, of course, degrees in length, and texture too, from the silky plumes of the Turkish Angora to the dense, deep ruffles of the Persian. But even the least shaggy longhair looks dramatically different from any shorthair.

The differences between the two, however, do not stop at the simple matter of shagginess. Under the fur of most – but not quite all – pedigree longhairs is an animal that is distinctly different in shape from its shorthair cousins. Starting at the head, a Persian cat should have a short, blunt nose set in a broad face. The eyes are large and wide open (slanting eyes would be a fault). The ears, with their handsome interior tufts, are rather small.

The large-boned body has a stocky, solid look; the breeder's aim is always to produce a cat that is massive without being clumsy. The tail is relatively short, and so are the legs – short, that is, compared with those of the average domestic cat with short fur. The Persian is, however, only one type of longhair. There are several other types and not all of them tend to this ideal of compact chunkiness.

In terms of overall shape, cats are divided into three main groups, of which the longhairs are one. It is, in fact, from the "average" domestic shorthair that the standards of perfection in the second group have been developed. In their pedigree form, the cats in this second group are known as the American, British and European shorthairs. Here again, the breeder aims to produce a compactly-shaped cat. But allied to this must go an impression of neat curves, strong muscles and a general readiness for action. The classic American shorthair has a straight, short nose, though not as short as that of a Persian. The head is big, the cheeks are plump and prominent, and the ears are medium-sized. As in the longhair, the eyes are round and wide open; any good domestic shorthair should have a characteristically alert, game-for-anything look. The neck is short, the chest powerful, and the legs and tail are of medium length. The fur is short, sleek and shining.

There are subtle differences between the American shorthair and its British and European relatives. The Old World breeds are cobbier, and more rounded, with slightly smaller ears and shorter legs and tail. A more radical difference exists between the American and a much newer form of shorthair, the Exotic. This is cobbier still than the British, and its fur is different too: less satiny and more velvety.

*Left:* At the moment, they're just little ones – but these two British Blue kittens will grow up to display the smooth curves and dense coat typical of the classic domestic shorthair breeds.

*Above:* A golden chinchilla Persian with all the beauty-marks of the type: wide face, small ears, massive build, big feet – and, of course, fur that is deep, soft and flowing.

71

The third main group of breeds is not quite as easy to recognize as the longhairs and the domestic shorthairs. All longhairs have long hair, and all the domestics have short coats. Most members of the third group also have short coats – but, in contrast, there are some with long, silky fur. One or two others have curly coats, and one – from Canada – is bald. In addition, some grow imposingly large, while others remain on the small side, and their temperaments range from the gentle to the overwhelming.

Despite these differences, however, all these cats have certain characteristics in common. Typically, their approach to life is lively and intelligent (at times over-intelligent, harried owners sometimes claim), and they all, within certain broad limits, have a similar shape. Everything about them is elongated and tapering; their faces, their bodies, their tails, even their eyes. There is nothing stocky or cobby about them.

## Siamese

The most famous member of this group is, of course, the Siamese. But the fact that the equally-loved Burmese is also a member shows just how wide the variations of body type within the group can be. A third member is called the Oriental or Foreign Shorthair, a cat that resembles a Siamese in shape but not in color. It would be perfectly possible to call the group to which they all belong after its best-known representative.

However, the word "Siamese" usually makes people think of a color pattern rather than a body type. The terms "oriental" and "foreign" do not have the same color connotations and are therefore commonly used to refer to the group as a whole. Most, though not all, of the members of this third group are usually thought of as oriental or foreign shorthairs.

The Oriental Shorthair itself is a cat with a Siamese-type body and a coat that is either patterned in a non-Siamese way or is of a solid (self) color. (This is according to the US definition; in Britain, the patterned cats are the Orientals, while the selfs are the Foreigns.)

## Slender shape

The overall shape to which the oriental or foreign lends its name is slender and refined. The nose is long and helps to give the head its characteristic wedge-like shape. The ears are large – enormous in the case of one of the curly-coated breeds, the Devon Rex. Neck, body and legs are all well-muscled but slender; the legs and tail are long, and the tail is tapering and whip-like.

Not all the breeds in the oriental group give the same highly streamlined impression. Some are more rounded and several have shorter noses. But the real odd ones out are different in yet another way: they have long fur. These "foreign longhairs" are the Balinese, the Somali and the Tiffany, which are the long-haired versions of, respectively, the Siamese, the Abyssinian and the Burmese. None of them, however, is shaped like the average longhair. Under their long coats, they all have the slender build of their shorthair relations.

*Below:* Halfway between the domestic shorthair and the true oriental, the Bombay is a Burmese hybrid. The breed's original parents were a Burmese and a black American Shorthair.

*Right:* Both this Siamese and Foreign White demonstrate the real oriental body type: big ears, pointed muzzle, slender limbs, and slanting eyes. The Siamese displays his whiplike tail.

While some doubt still hangs over the exact origins of the domestic cat, there is no doubt whatsoever that its ancestors were small, quiet-footed creatures that lived – like nearly all cats – by stalking their prey and then pouncing on it. But feather-light feet are not all a stalker (as opposed to a chaser) needs if it is to survive, and other requirements include the ability to melt into the background until the time comes for the final sprint. This calls for camouflage.

As shown at the other end of the feline spectrum by the tiger and the lion, stripes make an ideal camouflage in shadowy woodland, and so does a sandy, fawnish hide in sunny, scrubby open country. The cats that the ancient Egyptians domesticated were tabbies.

Amongst all the color categories that are used for feline classification, it is this same brown tabby – black markings on a brindled, grayish-fawn ground – that is the prototype.

Four distinct types of tabby exist today, of which the striped variety – also called mackerel or tiger – is the one that corresponds with the markings carried by the pre-domestic cat. However, this is now less often seen than the appropriately-named "classic" (or marbled, or blotched) pattern that we associate with the typical domestic cat watching life from the top of a wall.

In the third type, the dark bars are broken up, so that the overall effect is spotted rather than striped. The fourth is the Abyssinian, called after the breed of that name. The Abyssinian is often nicknamed the bunny cat, and this gives a clue to the reason for its inclusion in the tabby group. Like those of a wild colored rabbit, each hair of its coat is ticked, or marked with bands of a contrasting color. This ticked effect – for which the breeder's term is agouti – is present in the paler fur areas of all the tabby types; the special feature of the Abyssinian is that the dark overlying tabby bars have been almost bred out, except on the head.

*Above:* Bunny cat in the sun. The brindled coat of this relaxed Abyssinian has been caused by the presence of the agouti – or "ticked" – color gene in its hereditary make-up.

*Left:* Two silver tabbies. A classic (or blotched) tabby is on the left; the cat on the right shows the spotted effect produced by breaks in the tabby bars.

*Right:* A big brown tabby shorthair with all the markings he needs to pick up show points. The stripes across the chest are important, and so are those on the cheeks and legs.

At first sight, the average brown tabby seems a far cry from the jet-black Persian winning admiring glances on the show bench. At the same time, there seems little to connect the black Persian with its blue, chestnut or chocolate, and lavender or lilac counterparts elsewhere at the show. However, all the show cats do have something in common other than their breed or breeds: amazingly, all of them are really tabbies as well. Every single one bears stripes.

The answer to this conundrum lies in the workings of the genes that control cats' color. All cats possess the gene for agouti coloring, the brindled shade that allows tabby markings to show up. However, a mutant gene exists that cancels out the pale banding or ticking on normal, dark-tipped agouti fur, and in some cats the genes combine in such a way as to allow this "anti-agouti" mutation to make itself felt.

As a result, the brindled portions of the cat's fur turn into a solid dark color. Since, in the case of the brown tabby, the tabby marks are black to start with, the result is a black cat. Locked in its cells, it still has the genetic direction for tabbiness, but the characteristic markings are masked by the darkening of the surrounding fur.

## Mutations

The connection between the black cat and its blue, chestnut and lavender neighbors at the show is also a question of mutation. Odd though it may seem, the four colors are in fact "related". If they were being mixed in water-colors by a painter, they would all come from one single cake of paint. Black is the basic color, but – to take the paint-box comparison one stage further – it can be diluted.

*Above:* Black is one of the most important colors in the feline paintbox. But it's rare to find a totally black cat.

*Below:* A Russian Blue quivers with alertness. Blue is a genetically diluted form of black; blue cats are really grey.

Indeed, the geneticists' own term for the mutant gene that does the work here is "dilute", and the dilute form of black is the hazy bluish-gray shade that cat breeders know as blue. However, the color black can also be affected by further mutant genes to produce two shades of brown. These are called caramel/cinnamon and chestnut/chocolate. A final refinement comes when the gene for dilution is combined in the right way with either of the genes for brown coloring, the result being one of the two shades of soft pinkish-gray called lavender in the United States and lilac in Britain.

## Red shades

It is less of a surprise to find that all the red shades also group themselves into a single color family, this time governed by a gene labelled *O* for orange. However, the *O* gene has some peculiar qualities of its own. For instance, it is proof against the workings of the "anti-agouti" gene that should, in theory, give a cat a solid all-over color. So there are no truly solid reds, only red tabbies in which the tabby markings are as inconspicuous as the breeder can make them.

But the *O* gene's real idiosyncrasy lies in the fact that it is linked to its bearer's sex. The genetic make-up of female cats allows them to mix orange and black coloring and display the result as tortoiseshell. Males can be red or one of the black group of colors, but not both. The tortoiseshell tom is not, though, the creature of myth that many people think; they are born occasionally (the writers have known one), but they are almost always sterile. Since the dilute form of red is cream, cream cats are available in both sexes; however, blue-creams are another "female only" color variety.

*Below:* A Havana Brown and her kitten. The breed was started by a hybrid born of Siamese and black parents. There are in fact two Havana breeds, the US and the UK. The pair shown here are of the US type; the British Havanas look more Siamese.

*Above:* Not white, but white tipped with black, this chinchilla Persian (or Chinchilla) represents one of the most beautiful of all feline color types in the world.

*Below:* At the other end of the black-tipped spectrum, this black smoke shows its silver bleaching mainly on its ruff and its underparts.

Among the 12 genes that, between them, govern the feline color range, white is the winner that takes all. The potential for any other color, even the deepest black or the most persistent tabby, is swamped when it meets the all-powerful gene *W*. And even if two white cats' parents include a black and a tabby, the white pair will not, on average, have as many black and tabby offspring as could be expected.

Most of their kittens will, like them, be white – although these will carry the potential for the hidden color inside them, and this color can emerge if, say, a cat with a hidden "tabby" pattern mates with an ordinary tabby. Sometimes, too, tabby markings can be seen on kittens that will grow up pure white.

Given the power of the *W* gene, it is odd that the average domestic companion and cat-about-town is not white, but one of the more somber shades suited to camouflage. While the question of protective coloring is, of course, important in feral cat colonies, the main reason for this anomaly could lie elsewhere.

As all owners of pedigree whites know, the W gene can be accompanied by a tendency to deafness, especially in cats with blue eyes. The kittens affected become deaf soon after birth, and never regain their hearing. When a deaf female grows up and bears kittens of her own (most of which will be white), she is unable to react to their calls for food and help, and therefore makes a bad mother. The kittens, if they live, are likely both to be deaf themselves and to lack the intensive training in survival skills that their colored contemporaries have received. And so the cycle of deprivation continues. That is why a successful white is a triumph of both good luck and good management.

## Acute hearing

Pedigree whites have eyes that can be colored blue, orange, or one orange and one blue ("odd-eyed") and the tendency for deafness can, unfortunately, affect the orange and odd-eyed cats as well. However, there is one white breed whose hearing is as acute as its blue or green eyes are brilliant. This is the Foreign White, which is, in fact, an all-white Siamese. An Albino White also exists, in both domestic and foreign shorthair forms. This has pale blue eyes and, again, is free from hearing problems.

Although all-white cats seem to have a lot in common with the huge range of bi-colors – the black-and-whites, blue-and-whites, red-and-whites, everything-else-and-whites – the genetic make-up of these is actually quite different. It is a gene labelled *S* (for "spotting") that produces most bi-color coats, and its effect can range from a white dab on the paws and chin to an all-over white dazzle apart from patches on the ears and tail.

Show standards for bi-colors, however, exclude such extremes except in a few special cases (of which the Birman and the Turkish Van are two). The classic bi-color has no more than half its fur white, and the ideal is between half and one-third; attaining this ideal, however, is not easy.

## "Tipped" cats

Another color family that also appears to bear the *W* stamp consists of all the "tipped" cats: the cats whose pale fur shows a darker shade at the tips of each hair. Again, however, appearances are misleading, since the tipped effect is caused by yet a further gene known as the Inhibitor.

This works by inhibiting, or "bleaching out", a portion of the colored pigment on each hair of a non-white cat; only the tip then shows the cat's basic color. The extent to which the Inhibitor does its bleaching work can vary considerably, and it is these variations, com-

bined with the basic colors of black and red, that have given rise to the chinchilla, shaded and smoke color varieties, as well as the silver tabby. The golden chinchillas and shadeds are produced in a slightly different way, since they lack the Inhibitor. They really seem to be ultra-yellow agoutis, but their genetic make-up is still something of a mystery.

*Below:* Where patterns meet. A calico Persian like this one combines the genes for black and red with one for white spotting.

For all that a seal point Siamese looks as if it has waded in brown ink, its decorative markings do not derive from a genetic admixture of sepia to an otherwise pale cat. In fact, the reverse has happened: the seal point is basically a dark cat, and the gene that, in a different form, is responsible for producing albino felines, has worked here on the main part of the animal's body to reduce the dark coloring. Only the points – the legs, tail, ears and mask – retain the original dark color. Rather surprisingly, it is another gene of the albino family that produces the solid-color Burmese, removing any distinction between body color and points.

Since the "Siamese" gene works equally well on all colors, and on all types of cat, we have a large number of breeds that show the Siamese-style pattern, and a very large number of color varieties available.

One of the breeds – a longhair of the Persian type – is called the Himalayan, the name which is also used as a term to describe the Siamese-style coat pattern. (A Himalayan fancy rabbit, for example, also has dark paws, ears and nose.)

## Himalayan patterns

Another feature of the gene for Himalayan coloring is the way it affects eye color. In cats with the Himalayan pattern, the eyes are always blue, with the color ranging from the gentian-blue stare of the seal point to the softer delphinium shade of some of the paler varieties. The Burmese, of course, has golden eyes.

The reason why the gene for the Himalayan patterns works as it does can become apparent if a Siamese has to have some of its fur shaved. Many an owner of a spayed Siamese has looked at the dark new fur growing over the site of the operation and wondered how long this inelegant blotch would last. (In fact, it usually vanishes with the next molt.)

The cause of the temporary darkening is thought to be that the temperature of the shaved skin is slightly lower than that of the furred area – and the Himalayan-pattern gene works only on the warmer portions of the body. A cat's extremities are likewise cooler than the main part of its body, as anyone touching a cat's ears will know. The action of the gene is therefore blocked in these areas, and the dark points are formed.

*Above:* Unlike the cats opposite, this one is in fact a long-haired Siamese, or Balinese. This type of Siamese coloring, with tabby markings on face, paws and tail, is called lynx point.

*Right:* Siamese kittens at play. At this stage, the points have not yet attained their full extent and coloring. When newly born, Siamese kittens are white.

*Left:* Two Himalayans (Colorpoint Longhairs) in their full Persian-type glory. The cat on the left has blue points; the darker one on the right is a seal point.

How and where did the domestic cat first get long fur? Unfortunately, the name of the most celebrated of all the longhair breeds is less of a help than it sounds. Iran – Persia, as it was called – was indeed the point of origin of the first cobby, densely-furred long-haired cats to reach Europe. But these, though they were imported as early as the sixteenth century, were by no means the first of all longhairs to intrigue members of the French and Italian aristocracy.

The first arrivals came not from Persia, but from Turkey. Going further back, there is still another puzzle to be answered. Asia is also the home of one of the furriest of all wild cats, the manul or Pallas's cat of the steppes. So were some distant ancestors of the modern manul also the progenitors of our Persians and Angoras? It would be tempting to say so, but unfortunately there is little proof in favor of the theory.

Genetic changes can, of course, occur spontaneously anywhere in the world, and it is quite likely that every area that played host to the domestic cat also saw the emergence of a long-haired variant. In addition, shaggy cats will do better in a cold climate than their shorter-haired relatives, and when natural selection takes place their offspring will have a better chance of survival. So a cold climate is conducive to a shaggy breed of cat.

For these reasons, it is difficult to pinpoint the place, let alone the time, of the Persian's ultimate origin. All that can be said is that Asia, and in particular south-western Asia, seems a likely candidate.

*Left:* Once a queen's favorite, and still a top winner everywhere with breeders and owners, the blue Persian is one of the most imposing of all pedigree cats.

*Below:* The outlines of this young black Persian's body are all but hidden underneath the dense frills of its billowing coat. Its ruff has been brushed up to frame its face.

## European popularity

The European ancestors of the modern Persian took some time to catch up on their Turkish rivals in the popularity stakes. But catch up they did, and within 200 years of their arrival they were within sight of becoming the only popular image of what a long-haired cat should look like. Always prestigious pets to own, in the nineteenth century they added some very prestigious people to their list of fans.

Queen Victoria had her blue Persians and her son Bertie, later to become King Edward VII, patronized the Persian show ring (an example of the royal mother and son for once sinking their many differences in a shared interest). Around the same time the Persian travelled to the US and aroused as much admiration as it had done on the other side of the Atlantic.

## Color ranges

The color range in today's Persians includes all the basic solid colors and most of the patterns. There are whites (with blue eyes, copper or orange eyes, and odd eyes), blacks (with copper or orange eyes), blues (with copper or orange eyes) and creams (again with copper or orange eyes – these are, in fact, the favored eye colors for almost all the longhairs).

The tabbies are represented too, with a good silver tabby being particularly prized. (Unusually, eyes that are green or hazel are allowed.) The tortoiseshells are joined by the calicos (tortie-and-whites) and their color "cousins" the blue-creams and the dilute calicos (blue-cream-and-whites).

Another important group consists of the cats in which the Inhibitor gene has been at work: the chinchillas and shadeds. Here, breeders have used the color spectrums to produce a line of prizewinners that ranges from the pale shell cameo and the green-eyed chinchilla to the soot-and-silver black smoke.

In the US, all of these count as just one breed. Whatever their color, they are Persians first and foremost. In the UK, however, the situation is more complicated, since each color is accredited as a separate breed.

*Below:* The Peke-faced Persian has an even shorter nose than the classic Persian type. It is not favored in the UK.

*Left:* Two Siamese seal points with long fur? No; the only thing these cats have in common with the Siamese is the pattern of markings on their coats: dark on the face, ears, legs and tail, and paler elsewhere. In body type they are Persian, with small ears, broad faces, massive limbs and relatively short, thickly furred tails. In the United States they are called Himalayans, after the name given to this particular kind of coloring in many fancy livestock breeds; in the UK, they are Colorpoint Longhairs. Whatever their name, they always demonstrate a thick, fully Persian-type coat.

As with the Siamese, the Himalayan can be marked in a number of different colors, of which seal and blue are probably the best known. Others include red, tabby and tortoiseshell. Oddly enough, solid-colored cats of Himalayan origin also exist, and these – which come in the brown and lavender color ranges – are sometimes called Kashmirs.

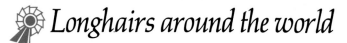
The city of Ankara or Angora has other claims to fame than as the capital of modern Turkey. Its name is connected with a particular sort of yarn, with goats, with rabbits – and with cats. The link between the Angora goat, its mohair, and the fluffiness of the Angora rabbit is an obvious one. It is interesting that Turkey's most famous contribution to the cat world should also be noted for its long and beautiful fur.

The Angora longhair made a considerable impression on upper-class Europe when it was first imported from Asia in the sixteenth century, and, even though it was later eclipsed by the more massive Persian, it could still claim some devoted admirers 300 years later. By then, however, it was losing ground very fast, and the process continued to the point where the big ears, long nose and tail, and light-boned body had lost all attraction whatsoever in the Persian-dominated world of the cat-fanciers of the nineteenth century.

## Turkish Angora

When interest finally revived in the US about 30 years ago, breeders had to re-import from the original home of the breed, Turkey itself, rather than work with existing stock. The result, formally called the Turkish Angora, demonstrates the flowing silky fur and rather slender build of its early namesakes. The fur owes part of its silky quality to the fact that it lacks the woolly undercoat of the Persian. Blacks, blues and some of the patterns are permitted, but pride of place in terms of both history and popularity goes to the whites.

In the UK, the Angora breed has a different background, being one that has been deliberately recreated through a planned series of matings. It does not carry the name "Turkish", this being the official British title of the Van cat.

The Angora – or something like it – was probably the cat that gave the gene for long hair to the ancestors of the best-known of the breeds created in the USA, the Maine Coon. In fact, the Maine Coon really created itself, although the story that its ancestors go back to a farm shorthair and a raccoon is merely a delightful myth.

*Below:* Clean-limbed and elegant, this snow-white Turkish Angora illustrates all the qualities that attracted both the cat-fanciers of four centuries ago and the breeders of the 1950s.

## Maine Coons

Maine Coons – their name contains memories of both the raccoon legend and the state thought to be their home – are big cats with large ears, noses on the long side and long, spectacularly bushy tails. Their fur is ideally suited to cold wind and weather, being smooth, thick and shaggy.

A tail is one thing that another northern longhair, the Cymric, conspicuously lacks, since this is a modern breed derived from the Manx. Like the Maine Coon, its country of origin is America and, although its fur is shorter than that of the "raccoon cat", the shape of its head is somewhat similar.

Also similar to the Maine Coon in build – and equipped with a tail as generously furred as the American's – is a cold-weather cat of the Old World, the Norsk Skaukatt. The Skaukatt's fur is even thicker, however, and its back legs are longer. A very old "natural" breed, it is known for its intelligence, its sociability, and the role it plays in Norwegian folk stories.

Given its character, it is obviously the main character in Scandinavia's own version of *Puss in Boots*. The villain in this is not the ogre of the better-known story but a troll – and, in folklore, trolls die in sunlight. So, to help her master (the cat in the Norwegian story is female), resourceful Puss keeps the troll chatting all through the night, letting the morning sun destroy him.

*Below:* The Norsk Skaukatt, or Norwegian Forest Cat. Big, bold and handsome, it looks a match for anybody, even the trolls and monsters of Scandinavian folklore.

*Right:* A silver tabby Maine Coon, showing off its characteristically big ears with their attractive tufts. The M on the forehead is a classic mark of tabby beauty.

One of the most charming of the longhairs is the Birman, or the Sacred Cat of Burma. Among those who don't know it, however, it is also a great source of confusion, for its name carries a misleading reminder of the quite distinct Burmese, and its coloring is similar to that of the Himalayan.

On meeting a Himalayan lookalike that still doesn't look quite right, the rule is to look at the feet. In the Himalayan – as in the Siamese – they will be darker than the main body fur. But the fur on a Birman's feet will not merely be paler than that of the body; it will be pure snow white. On the back feet, the white will extend part of the way up the cat's "heels", or hocks. These white gloves are the main hallmark of the breed.

Less conspicuously different, perhaps, but equally distinctive is the cat's build. The Birman is low-slung and long-bodied; however, it is not as short in the leg as the Persian or Himalayan, and the body is slimmer. The face is different too: the nose is long and slightly Roman, and the ears are relatively big. As a result, the Birman has a rather brisk, wideawake look not seen among cats of the Persian type. True, the eyes are large and round, almost in Persian style, but their color is a true Siamese blue of great intensity and charm.

## Mixture of influences

The coat shows a similar mixture of influences; while long, it is silky rather than fluffy in the classic Persian manner. The white feet apart, the breed is marked in the Siamese manner and in some of the colors accepted for the Siamese. In the US the basic pale body color is expected to be lighter than it is in the UK and Europe.

Among the many legends that surround the origins of the various feline breeds, that of the Birman is one of the most elaborate. Its theme is indicated by the cat's other name, for, so the legend runs, the breed's founder was a white Burmese temple cat called Sinh. Sinh was one of a company of 100 white cats that, much like their opposite numbers in ancient Egypt, lived in the temple of the goddess Tsun-Kyan-Kse, where they did her honor and kept the priests company. Sinh was the particular cat of an aged priest called Mun-Ha.

## Birman legend

One night while Mun-Ha was praying before the statue of the goddess – a golden statue with eyes of fabulous sapphires – bandits broke into the temple and killed him. Fiercely protective, his devoted cat leapt on to his body. The minute its feet touched the old man's white hair, they turned white as well. In the shine of the golden statue, its body took on a golden tinge, while its face and legs turned a dark sable brown. And, as Sinh's eyes began to glow as blue as the goddess's own, the soul of the good Mun-Ha entered his pet's body.

Sinh himself died seven days later, taking the priest's soul with him to Heaven. But, on that day, all the other temple cats were blessed with Sinh's holy coloring, and from then onwards they and their descendants were venerated for the holiness they so clearly shared.

Although the legend is a beautiful one, the truth may be more prosaic. It was in France that the Birman breed was first recognized between the two World Wars. It may have been founded by cats that came from southeast Asia, if not Burma itself, but it may also be a breed actually created in Europe, like the Himalayan it resembles so closely. The really odd thing is that, even though the breed emerged well within living memory, no one seems to be sure where the truth lies.

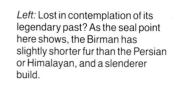

*Left:* Lost in contemplation of its legendary past? As the seal point here shows, the Birman has slightly shorter fur than the Persian or Himalayan, and a slenderer build.

*Right:* Whatever the facts about their origins, the Birmans of today are quite at home in the ordinary world of food, sleep, shows – and mountaineering in ornamental rock-gardens.

All cats hate water – or so we tend to think. But do they? Of course, an enforced bath (with shampoo) is seldom very pleasant for a cat, but there are some who show no particular rush to come in when it is raining. In the wild, too, there is a small group of cats that depend to a considerable extent on water for their food or their well-being; the tiger, which enjoys a dip, is both the best-known and the largest. And, back in the world of the domestic cat, there is one pedigree breed that enjoys a dip just as much: the red and white cat from Asia Minor that is known as the Turkish Van, or the Van in the US and the Turkish in Britain.

## White blaze

It is named after the great bitter lake in eastern Turkey. This breed first arrived in the west soon after the Second World War, when breeders began to rediscover the elegant charm of the older, more slender longhair type, the Angoras. Indeed, the Van really is a type of Angora, though it is a lot cobbier in outline. What marks it out

from its fellow-Turk is its coloring and temperament. The "Van pattern" is strictly defined, and consists of red patches on the face and a red, ringed tail. All the rest of the coat should be chalk-white, although small random patches of red are allowed on the body. An important accent is a well-defined white "blaze" down the forehead to between the eyes.

The Van came to the United States and Europe equipped with a reputation as a voluntary swimmer, and this reputation has been borne out. Photographic evidence exists of the Van striking out fearlessly through the water, while the pictures on these pages show another aspect of its liking for being wet.

*Below:* Special swimming sessions for two Turkish Van cats. While the owners' hands are ready in case of problems, the cats don't seem worried. Both show the markings of the breed.

*Right:* While Van cats know a lot about water, this one is more than a little bemused by all those bubbles.

Among all the issues involved in cat breeding, the question of national – and frequently continental – preference is one of the most fascinating. Within several of the major breeds, quite marked differences exist between the ideals aimed at on either side of the Atlantic, and there are further differences between different localities on each continent.

The contrast between the perfect US Burmese and the perfect UK one is possibly the most obvious example of distinctive national taste, but US preferences do seem to tend overall to a more rounded, chunky animal. However, the case of one of the very oldest of all the US breeds is among the exceptions to this general rule about the chunkiness of American cats.

Put a pedigree American Shorthair side by side with its British or European counterpart, and the difference is immediately apparent. The American is without doubt the more lightly-built cat. Its slimmer neck gives its head a more upright, "high-collared" pose than the Britisher, and it also has a longer, slightly narrower face, and taller ears.

## Coat requirements

The American's impression of height is increased by its greater leg length, and this is echoed at the cat's rump by a longer tail. For both the US and the UK, however, the coat requirements are the same: short, dense and shining. Any tendency to fluffiness is a fault, as is a snub nose in the Persian style.

Although the pedigree American Shorthair mainly derives from all the ordinary domestic shorthairs that, through US history, helped pioneer farmers and their descendants with their vermin problem, it is not quite the oldest US breed in the book. It was the shaggy-coated and more distinctive Maine Coon that came in at the head of the line when the US cat fancy started to establish itself last century. The American Shorthairs' early history as a distinct breed was also complicated by an admixture of British Shorthair blood.

Now, however, the type is clearly distinct – and secure – enough for deviations from it to be welcomed and encouraged rather than rejected as genetic mistakes. Proof of this is given by the remarkable success of a fledgling breed that, in one respect, departs in the most revolutionary manner possible from the standard of not only the American Shorthair itself but also from that of almost all catdom: the aptly-named American Wirehair.

The first Wirehair of all was born only twenty years ago, in 1966; he was a red and white mutant called Adam, whose fur defied all known rules for cats and was crisply scrunched and crinkled. The breed won official acceptance a decade later.

*Above:* Meet the British Shorthair, in this case a calico (called tortoiseshell and white in the UK). All outlines are rounded, the cheeks are full, and the build is definitely chunky.

*Left:* Just like an ordinary American Shorthair in all respects – except one. The American Wirehair is one of the newest breeds to emerge in the cat fancy world.

*Right:* In contrast to its British opposite number (top right), this beautifully marked silver tabby American Shorthair shows off its "high-collared" look and alert, upright stance.

Powerfully-built, pleasingly solid, and as smooth as silk velvet, the British Shorthair and its European cousin have a distinct appeal of their own. They are, of course, everyone's basic idea of a cat; indeed, the picture a young child learns to draw with a couple of coins could be a portrait of a prizewinning Britisher, compact and rounded. But however "ordinary" a pedigree British Shorthair may look, its appearance is the product of just as much care and forethought on the part of its breeder as that of any Persian or Siamese.

## Common characteristics

The classic British Shorthair is more massively built than its American opposite number. Its neck is thicker, its head and face are more rounded, and its legs and tail are shorter. The chest is deep and powerful, and so is the rest of the body. The wide-apart ears are slightly smaller than the American's; in both breeds, however, the eyes are large and widely-opened. Another characteristic the breeds share is neat, rounded feet; when, in the world of dog breeding, greyhound owners talk of "cat feet", it is of the domestic shorthair's paws that they are thinking. All these characteristics are shared by the European Shorthair which, to all intents and purposes, is the same breed as the British.

All the solid colors are permitted, plus the various types of tabby (including the spotted), and the smokes, and the other Inhibitor-produced tones. Cats in the chinchilla or cameo color ranges are called the British Tipped. Naturally, the tortoiseshell family of colors is well-represented too.

The most famous color variety of all, however, is the blue. Dignified in its home country by the special breed name of British Blue, this best-loved of the British shorthair breeds has the soft color of its fur set off by the glowing orange of its big eyes. Interestingly, a slightly different blue shorthair used to claim similar top honors for France: this is the Chartreux, named after the Carthusian monks who allegedly first bred it. Its fur has a more silvered look than that of the British, with which it has now often been interbred.

The Exotic Shorthair is a breed that looks something like the British but is, in fact, American. Descended from shorthair/Persian crosses, it is even more rounded and cobbier in outline than its transatlantic cousin (which, at one point, was also classed by some US cat fancy bodies as an Exotic). The most obvious reminder of its Persian parentage is the snub nose, much shorter than that of the ordinary domestic shorthair; another is the soft, full coat, dense and velvety (plush-like).

*Left:* A classic example of his breed, Grand Champion Brynbuboo Bosselot – a British Shorthair – stares challengingly at the camera. Everything about this brown spotted tabby is majestic: shape, expression, even the pose of the neatly-rounded feet.

*Right:* The British Shorthair in its most famous color variety. In its home country, the British Blue is a breed in its own right, and demonstrates to perfection the ideal British shape.

At the moment the great flood came, Noah, so they say, panicked and slammed the doors of the Ark on two of his passengers' tails. Alternatively, the Celtic warriors in the cats' homeland prized those same long tails as helmet-crests; a crisis was approaching when the female cats took matters into their own jaws and docked their kittens' tails at birth. Alternatively again, the cats came to their home in the Irish Sea from points as various as Spain and Japan – far-flung foreign parts, either way, full of prodigies and marvels . . .

The breed in question is, of course, the Manx, whose high, rounded rump ends not in a tail or even in a stump, but in a small hollow where the tail should start. That, at least, is the standard of perfection, but it is not often achieved because of the special problems that beset the breeding of the Manx. A breeder specializing in these animals has to be a patient one.

*Below:* Another cat with a briskly alert look, the Japanese Bobtail appears in no way disadvantaged by any genetic problems connected with its odd tail structure. Red is a favorite Bobtail color, especially when combined with black and white.

## The perfect match

The (relatively) simple matter of mating a near-perfect female to a near-perfect male is complicated by the cat's genetic make-up to the extent that the Manx specialist scarcely knows what to expect until the female actually produces the litter. The trouble is that the special Manx gene – the direction given to the developing body to omit a tail – carries what is known as a lethal factor.

A "double dose" of this gene, which a proportion of all embryos from a Manx-to-Manx mating must have, kills the embryos affected in the womb. So any Manx kitten that is born is, in effect, a mongrel as far as the Manx element goes; its gene for taillessness is paired with one that directs the embryo to grow a normal tail. Because the Manx gene is dominant, the kitten's tail will be shorter than normal – but precisely because the kitten is a mongrel, it is difficult to predict precisely how short.

Cats that carry the Manx gene can have vestigial tails, short tails, and even quite long tails, as well as no tails at all. The three types with tails are known as rumpy-risers, stubbies (stumpies in the UK) and longies. The truly tailless Manx is a rumpy.

## Spinal disorders

Genetically, all of these are crossbreeds as far as tailless-ness goes – and, for this reason, they can pass on the life-saving direction for a normal tail that cancels the worst effect of the Manx gene. (For the same reason, a proportion of their kittens will have perfectly ordinary tails.) Even if the stubbies and the rest are no use for show purposes, they are still liked by breeders because, along with the potential for taillessness, they can hand on the other Manx characteristics of long back legs, big ears and a soft, thick coat. With these characteristics, however, goes a less desirable tendency – again the product of the gene for taillessness – to suffer from serious spinal disorders.

Another breed that differs dramatically from the norm, and that also has a potential genetic problem built in, is the Scottish Fold. The Fold is even more unmistakable in outline than the Manx, for its ears fold forward and over to give the effect of a tight little cap.

The first cat recorded to have this peculiarity – a female called Susie – appeared in 1961 on a Scottish farm. Susie and her kittens – two of whom also had folded ears – became the founders of the breed, which at first looked likely to have a future in both the UK and the US. However, it was noticed that folded ears seemed to be accompanied in some cats by bone abnormalities. There were also fears that the folded ears themselves might lead to problems, and the breed was not accepted in Britain.

As far as it is known, no such genetic troubles affect a third breed of cats with a shape unique among felines. This is the attractive Japanese Bobtail, whose short tail stump is concealed by a neat puff of fur. Lightly-built and silky to the touch, the Bobtail is a very old breed in its native Japan, but it was not introduced to the United States until the late 1960s.

*Above:* Like all members of its breed, this bi-color Scottish Fold has a startling resemblance to a little dog. But the big eyes and neat muzzle are totally cat-like.

*Below:* A Manx in a hurry. It has no problem balancing its way along the gate – although, if an ordinary cat were to lose its tail, it could take weeks to adjust to the loss.

At a period when Europe was still deep in the Middle Ages, a poet in the brilliant Siamese capital of Ayudha turned to the eighth feline in the list that he was elegantly cataloging. Its name was Diamond; its ears, muzzle, tail and legs were black, while the rest of its body was white. Its eyes had a reddish-orange glow. Physiologists will nod their heads at the accuracy of this description of what happens when light is reflected back from the blue eyes of the typical foreign shorthair.

In all the other details Siamese owners will instantly recognize the most striking characteristic of their pets. Ayudha fell to invaders in the eighteenth century, but the poems survived – and so, of course, did the cats, which are equally beautiful.

## Origins

Although the evidence of the *Cat-Book Poems* gives excellent grounds for concluding that the Siamese cat really is a Siamese breed, it is not so helpful on the question of whether the breed originated in Siam in the first place. The "Himalayan" pattern has been observed in cats elsewhere in the world, notably – and first – by the naturalist Peter Pallas in the late 1700s. On his epic journey across Russia to the Far East, Pallas noticed a rather small cat, brownish in color, with black ears, feet and tail and additional black on the face.

Amidst all the mysteries, however, one thing is certain: the first Siamese to reach the UK really did come from Siam, now Thailand. They arrived in Europe around the time that the cat finally re-established itself as a pet, and appeared at the famous 1871 cat show at Crystal Palace organized by Harrison Weir. In fact – and for all that the climate of opinion was by then running firmly in cats' favor – this ornamental new breed from the romantic Orient almost failed to survive transplantation to the west.

Although the cats were not nearly as extreme in appearance as a modern Siamese, they were still regarded askance by many – much, one imagines, as the Scottish Fold or the Rex were in some quarters when they first came on the scene. Furthermore, the Siamese seemed worryingly delicate in the cold, damp climate of north-western Europe.

However, a sufficient number of dedicated owners and breeders fell under the Siamese spell to persevere and, by the beginning of the new century, the breed's British future seemed assured. By this time, too, the Siamese had started its highly successful conquest of the United States.

*Below:* As these two lynx point Siamese show, cats are just as capable of devoted friendships as other domestic animals.

*Below right:* The first warm sunshine of the year. Which are the bluer: the spring flowers or the eyes of this seal point?

## Quick change

It is startling to think that, today, those first Siamese would find themselves bottom of their class in any show. The changes that have taken place in the cats' bodies, let alone their color, are a striking illustration of how much the forces of evolution can be speeded up once man starts taking a hand. (Whether such speed is a good thing is, of course, another matter. In natural evolution it is survival that determines matters: in breeding, it is man.)

By today's standards, the early Siamese were far too rounded, too solid, and often too dark. Their tails had the famous kink near the tip and, even worse, their eyes squinted. The Siamese squint is, in fact, caused by a genetic fault in the breed's ocular nerves; now, however, this tendency has almost been bred out of show animals, and the same is true of the kink.

Although, unusually, the US favors a more elongated body type than do the British and Europeans, the definition of the perfect modern Siamese is both well-known and very straightforward. The cats should have a long, fine-boned face, broad at the ears and narrow at the muzzle; large ears, set wide apart; a slender neck; a slender and well-muscled body; long, slim legs, ending in small oval feet; and a long, finely-tapered tail. The eyes are "oriental" (slightly slanting) in shape, and piercingly blue. The fur is very short and smooth.

## Choice of colors

Although the correct body type for a Siamese is easy to sum up, the same is not true for the permitted color range. Hardly a year seems to go by, indeed, without some new color for the "points" being conceived as a possibility, or developed, or stabilized, or accepted somewhere in the world as a genuine new color variety. (Often, the first inspiration is given to the breeder by the sight of the mongrel kittens a Siamese queen has contrived to produce.)

The basic and longest-accepted colors are seal (a deep, sooty brown), blue, mid-brown and frost/lilac. To these, in the 1930s and 1940s, breeders began to add the red tones; with the result that points became available in red, cream, tortoiseshell and blue-cream.

It was a Siamese herself who, in the traditional feline way, laid the foundation for the lynx (tabby) points, and these are available in the full range of seal, blue, chestnut brown, lavender and tortoiseshell. Meanwhile, points with the dark tipping produced by the Inhibitor gene are also now being produced, with New Zealand in particular taking a pioneering role.

Just to add to these complexities, cats with points in some of these colors – notably the reds and tabbies – are grouped as Colorpoint or Colorpoint Shorthairs rather than Siamese. But that only holds true of the US; in Britain, they are all accepted as Siamese color variants.

Although popular taste ended by rejecting the dark-furred Siamese that accompanied its lighter cousin to Europe in the early days, it was nevertheless a cat of this darker type that gave rise to a breed that has become as popular as the Siamese itself. The breed did, in fact, already exist in its native south-east Asia, but the author of the Siamese *Cat-Book Poems* would not in all probability have given the brown cats he drew and described the name "Burmese", for to him they were quite simply "brown cats".

The founder of the Burmese breed was a mink-colored Siamese, Wong Mau, which San Francisco cat enthusiast Dr. Joseph C. Thompson acquired on a visit to Rangoon in 1930. Wong Mau was a typical dark Siamese, with a brown body and darker brown points, and she would today be classed as a Tonkinese. Genetically, "Tonks" are a Burmese/Siamese hybrid, a fact that became apparent when Dr. Thompson, intrigued by Wong Mau's appearance, devised an experimental breeding program for her. She was first mated to a Siamese, and her litters were mated to each other and to herself.

Initially, the results were either Siamese or Tonkinese in appearance, but breeding attention given to the darkest of the Tonks started to produce a cat of foreign type that was dark brown all over – the first Burmese to be born in the West.

The rich glossy sable brown of those prototypes is still the traditional color for the Burmese today. However, a blue Burmese soon appeared (with a grayer coat than in the blue varieties of other breeds) and it was inevitably followed within a few generations by chestnut/chocolate and lavender/lilac variants.

Inevitably, too, complications over labelling developed. In the US (though not in Britain), the non-sables are sometimes, but not always, called Malayans. Again, the US names for the chestnut and lavender hues are respectively champagne and platinum. Other colors keep on being added to the list of those permitted. But the greatest variation of all concerns something more fundamental: the shape of the perfect Burmese head.

Very distinct differences exist here between US standards and those of the UK and Europe. While the face of the Old World cat has something of the oriental "wedge", the American's head is more apple-shaped: nicely rounded and full. Again, in a UK brown Burmese, the golden eyes are almond-shaped, whereas in an American cat they should be round.

These curving, rounded outlines are also a hallmark of the head and eyes of another Burmese color variant which has achieved independent breed status: the black Bombay. Bombays are, in fact, hybrids, since they originated in a Burmese/American Shorthair cross, with the shorthair contributing the jet-black coat.

*Above:* A free-ranging blue Burmese surveys its territory. The blues are among the longest-established of the Burmese color varieties; they are sometimes called blue Malayans.

*Right:* The cream Burmese is a much newer arrival. However, it shares its active, inquisitive temperament with all other members of the breed. This one is watching a bee.

*Left:* Halfway house? The modern Tonkinese breed results from Siamese/Burmese crosses and some of this cat's kittens will look like Burmese or Siamese cats. Wong Mau, founder of the Burmese breed, was really a Tonkinese.

With the other oriental or foreign shorthairs, international confusion over names and standards perhaps reaches its ultimate. In the US, the group as a whole are known as orientals; in Britain, however, they are known as foreigns – unless they are patterned.

In both countries, therefore, the oriental group is the right place for the US Egyptian Mau and the rather different Mau of the UK (now called the Oriental Spotted Tabby). If you switch over to the "foreign" label, it is also the right group for the British Havana, once called the Chestnut Brown Foreign and, before that, the Havana again. But the American Havana Brown looks radically dissimilar to its transatlantic counterpart and scarcely belongs in the oriental group at all . . .

Obviously, it would be a brave man or woman who produced an effective scheme to rationalize this jumble. However, the ordinary cat-lover can perhaps be forgiven for feeling that someone ought to try.

## Color problem

Much of the problem seems to arise from the huge number of colors now available within the Oriental/Foreign Shorthair breed itself. This runs the full gamut from ebony (black in the UK) to white, taking in the browns,

blues, lavenders, reds and red-derivatives on the way. The issue of which colors can compete in which show classes depends on the country where the show is held. Tabbies are allowed, and called orientals in Britain rather than foreigns, while tipped and shaded orientals are also being developed.

Often the names given to all these various hues on different sides of the Atlantic are, if not identical, at least self-explanatory. The real trouble sets in when the names are similar but – as in the case of the Havana – they describe very different animals. The Havana Brown has a characteristically "stopped" profile and is altogether more rounded than its sinuous British counterpart. The Britisher, whose lines of descent are not the same, is a Siamese-type cat with a long head.

Happily, things are easier with two other oriental-type shorthairs that, while sharing the same color, have different histories, different shapes, and different names to match. One is the Russian Blue and the other is the Korat.

*Below:* Covered in best plush. Although it looks like a "hot weather" cat, the slender-limbed

Russian Blue is equipped with a coat that will turn the worst of northern winters.

## Russian Archangel

The Russian Blue supposedly originated in the port of Archangel, just south of the Arctic Circle. Whatever the truth of this, its fur, though short, is supremely well-equipped to protect it from the cold, since it is very soft, dense and close in texture.

The general impression is of a cat covered in the finest silvery-blue plush – and, just like plush, the fur can be stroked both ways without disturbing its nap. The eyes are green; rounded in the US, almond-shaped in Britain. The cat's general outline is slim and refined, and its head has a very distinctive, rather short-muzzled shape. The whisker pads are particularly noticeable. Australia has made a special contribution to the Russian Blue's future, for there the breed now has a companion in the shape of a Russian White.

The Korat, which is also built on slender lines, is a Siamese breed of great antiquity, but there its resemblance to its more famous compatriot stops. It has nothing of the extreme elongation of the modern Siamese, and the shape of its head, like that of the Russian Blue, is unique. The ears are big, the cheeks curved and the chin small and pointed; the overall effect is usually described as "heart-shaped." The round green eyes are huge; the smooth blue coat has an even more silvery tinge than that of the Russian, and derives its shimmering look from a silver tip to each hair.

*Above and below:* Black, brown... and lavender. The ebony Oriental Shorthair on its straw mat shows the true oriental type; the Havana Brown and her kittens are "modified" orientals.

Abyssinians are among top athletes of the cat world. They are tireless runners, leapers and climbers; some will even play retrieving games with their owners as long as the "ball" is something they can pick up.

Although broadly oriental in type, Abyssinians are more solidly built than the Siamese or Oriental Shorthair. The face is less wedge-shaped than that of the Siamese, and the ears are smaller – although their height is often increased by little tufts of the ear-tips, rather like those of a squirrel or a lynx. The breed gets its overall brindled look from the bands of ticking on each hair in the Abyssinian coat: about two or three in the case of the Abyssinian itself, and up to a dozen in the related Somali (see overleaf). There are two color varities, ruddy (or normal) and sorrel, which is much redder in tone.

Until comparatively recently, the idea of an oriental longhair would have been a contradiction in terms. Longhairs were longhairs – big, fluffy, large-boned Persians – and orientals were the slender Siamese and its fellows. However, the mutant gene for long hair is no respecter of breed standards, and it was only to be expected that long-haired kittens should from time to time turn up in the best-run oriental households.

As interest in cats and cat breeding grows – and, as the preceding pages show, it is growing at an ever-increasing rate – breeders and the public are rejecting the old "it's no good, so get it neutered" approach. Instead, they are becoming more and more willing to bring an unbiased eye to the newcomers, and to acknowledge the attractions they possess.

### Spectacular Balinese

So far, three oriental breeds have produced long-haired variants that are winning acceptance as breeds. Of the three, the Balinese developed by US breeders is perhaps the most spectacular, combining as it does the Siamese markings of its parents with a long, close-lying, silky coat of the Angora type. (Indeed, in Britain, crosses with Angoras are used to reinforce the coat quality.).

Unlike the Himalayan/Colorpoint Longhair, it can truly be called a long-haired Siamese, since the fur conceals a slim, elegant body of the Siamese type. The points can be in the usual wide range of colors open to the Siamese, with the proviso that US Balinese which are not marked in seal, blue, chestnut or lavender must be classed as Javanese.

The second oriental longhair is the Somali, the dense-furred cousin of the Abyssinian. Both ruddy and sorrel (known as "normal" and "red" respectively in the UK) versions are available, and both types can have as many as twelve bands of ticking on each hair of their long coats. Both, too, share the modified oriental type of the short-haired version, and display their ear tufts as an additional mark of beauty.

The third member of the group derives from the Burmese, and is called the Tiffany. It has the rich brown coat of the sable Burmese, only in a paler tone.

*Below:* Unlike the Himalayan, the Balinese really is a Siamese cat with long fur. Under the silky coat, this cat has the fine bones and slender body of a classic Siamese.

*Right:* Like the Balinese, the long-haired version of the Abyssinian – the Somali – has breed status in its own right. A small white patch is permitted under the chin.

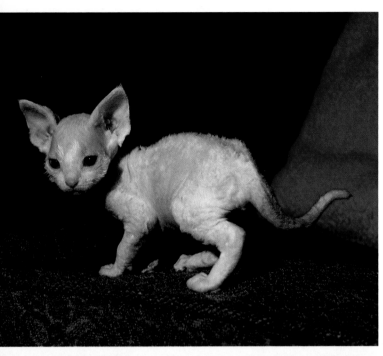

It is in the Rex cats – the Cornish, the Devon, the now-lost Ohio and Oregon, the German, and the recently-emerged Dutch – that the possibilities for genetic mutation among felines are seen to possibly their most dramatic effect. Until the 1940s, isolated cats with curly coats were creatures of semi-legend, reported here and there but difficult to trace. Between 1946 and 1960, however, everything changed.

It is now possible to breed, show and buy curly-coated cats in a huge variety of colors and patterns, including (in Britain but not in the United States) Siamese points in their equally wide variety of tones. Experiments have also been made in breeding longhairs with curly coats; so far, the results appear not to have been encouraging, but this does not mean that a curly-coated longhair will never win approval. The only constant – so far – is the cats' body type. This is uniformly foreign, though only moderately so in the case of the Cornish Rex and its identical German form. The more extreme Devon also stands out from the others by virtue of the unique shape of its head.

*Top left:* As this five-week-old kitten demonstrates, the Devon Rex's reputation for a pixie appearance is well-deserved. Its ears will continue to dominate its looks – although not quite to this extent.

*Left:* An adult Devon Rex, showing off its rippling coat, big ears, and short, brittle whiskers. Although the fur looks like that of the Cornish Rex opposite, the two breeds are genetically quite distinct.

## Cornish rival

The German was the first curly-coated cat to draw attention to itself. Its circumstances were hardly propitious to its survival, let alone its adoption and rise to fame; it was a feral cat living in the devastated city of Berlin immediately after the Second World War. However, rescued it was, and given the delightful name of Lämmchen (lambkin). But, by then, its claim to uniqueness had suddenly been destroyed by a cream kitten born to a farm cat in Cornwall, England. Called Kallibunker, this curly chance-born attracted great attention among breeders and geneticists and his descendants became the founders of the curly-coated new breed in both Britain and America. The breed was named the Rex, after the Rex fancy rabbit. As in the rabbit, the fur of the Cornish Rex cat lacks long guard hairs; the curly rippling coat we see is, in fact, the cat's undercoat.

Like the German before him, Kallibunker and his offspring did not retain their unrivalled importance for long. Nine years after Kallibunker's birth, another curly kitten was born to a stray sheltering under a garden hedge in the neighboring county of Devon. The owner of the garden rescued the mother and her family and, on noticing the unusual fur of one of the kittens, was as intrigued by the discovery as the Cornish kitten's owner had been earlier. The novelty – another male, dark gray and named Kirlee – joined the Rex breeding program when he became adult, and confounded everybody by siring kittens that, one and all, had straight coats.

Eventually, the answer emerged: the breeders were dealing with not one genetically distinct breed of Rex cat, but two. The Devon breed has a slightly different coat, and Kirlee, founder of his line, has also bequeathed to his descendants his unusually shaped profile with its pronounced stop. This, combined with the big eyes and ears, give the Devon Rex its "pixie" look.

*Below:* An imposing Cornish Rex. Most solid colors are allowed in both breeds of Rex, along with most patterns. As shown here, the Cornish Rex head is less extreme in outline than the Devon.

# 5 CAT CHAMPIONS

Not every cat can carry off the trophies and rosettes at a show of champions – and not every cat's owner is prepared or able to devote to showing the time and patience that is necessary to win top honors. But every cat can have his day – whether it's in the tense excitement of the show hall, notching up another mouse in the woodshed, or an invigorating session of "killing" a ball of paper in a corner of the lounge. There is scope for championship of all kinds in the world of the cat – not forgetting, of course, the possibility that even if you can't be a champion yourself, you can bear and nurture one.

Surrounded here by the trophies it has won, a chinchilla with its silvered coat is poised for further victories. But even champions do get drowsy – sometimes!

Both cat and owner need a good deal of experience if they are to be successful at showing, and it is as well for the owner to realize at the beginning that, although showing is an absorbing and fascinating pastime, it is also a time-consuming one which only the real enthusiast can sustain.

The first obvious step is for the owner to go to as many shows as possible and observe at first hand the peak of perfection that the winners attain. It is helpful for a beginner to take some cat-knowledgeable friend along, because the sight of so many admirable cats in such profusion can be meaningless unless one knows what to look for.

### Getting experience
In theory, at least, judges award points up to a maximum number for each physical feature – eye color, coat, and so on – but the overall impression is paramount. Most shows have classes for non-pedigree cats, sometimes including special classes for child owners, and here the overall impression is everything: the judges are looking for a handsome cat that is clearly loved and well looked after. This is as good a way as any for an owner who is thinking of rearing pedigree kittens for show to get some experience.

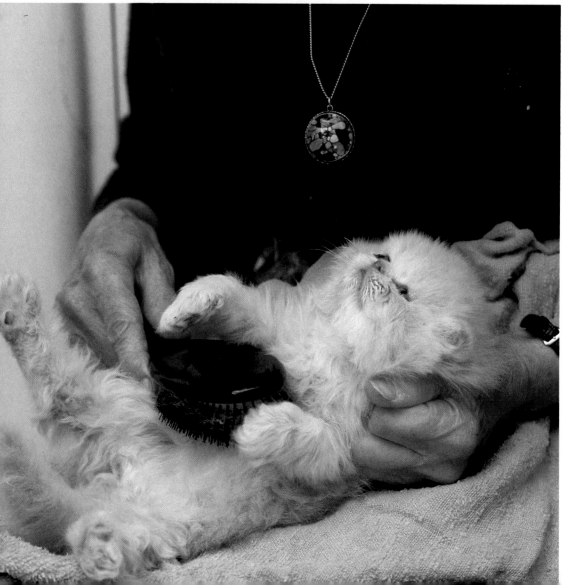

*Top left:* Getting ready for the show. This young odd-eyed white does not look too happy about his bath – but white coats do present a problem in cats that have got to look their best.

*Left:* Shows are still in the future – but preparations start early with potential champions. This kitten is cheerfully growing accustomed to its daily grooming session.

*Right:* The preparations were worth it. An orange-eyed white Persian, with flowing coat and massive dignity, considers the tributes paid to him.

Preparing a cat for showing is not merely a question of attention to its appearance. The conditions of a show are highly unnatural, and cats have to be trained to them. Your show cat must be used to sitting quietly for a long period in a pen, and to being inspected and handled by a large number of people. Most cats, with training and experience, accept this equably enough, but there is the occasional rebel who, despite everything, will not play. In this case, there is simply nothing to be done, and you must rule out showing this particular cat. Fortunately, getting a cat used to being penned and handled is something that can easily be done at home – rebels apart – if you use a dummy pen and as many of your family, neighbors and friends as are willing to help.

## Star grooming
Grooming for a show cat is more detailed and frequent than for the ordinary domestic pet. Both comb and brush should be used, in that order, followed, for the shorthairs, by a final stroking with a chamois leather or a pad of silk. In the case of longhairs, the frill or ruff must be brushed up so as to frame the face. The legs must be kept free of tangles. Include – as always when grooming any cat – an inspection of the mouth for discolored teeth or gums, checking for bad breath.

Inspect the base of the tail for "stud tail" – a greasy, scurfy condition which, despite its name, is not confined to entire toms. The prescribed treatment is regular washing with soapy water, taking care to rinse and dry the area thoroughly.

Powder may be used on light-colored longhairs as a dry shampoo. Special grooming powders are available, but unperfumed talcum powder or corn starch are just as effective, and less expensive. The coat should be opened by lightly brushing from tail to head, and the powder is then sprinkled on and worked in gently with the fingers. It should be left for a few minutes to give it time to absorb dirt and grease, and must then be *completely* brushed and combed out. The coats of dark-colored longhairs may be treated with bay rum, sprinkling a few drops on a pad of absorbent cotton and working methodically. Dry afterwards with a fresh pad for a deep, sparkling condition.

Cats entered for pedigree breed classes at any show must, of course, be registered members of their breed. It is essential, too, that their vaccination certificates are up to date at the time of the show; and it is only fair to other breeders – to say nothing of your cat – to cancel your show plans if your entry is ailing in any way on the show day itself.

*Left:* A show champion? Or a champion mouser? Or just a champion cat – strong, alert, ready to cope with whatever comes his way and turn it to his advantage? This beautiful mackerel or striped red tabby, with his deep orange eyes, could be all three. A British Shorthair, he is cobbier than his American cousin, with slightly smaller ears and shorter tail.

*Above:* They're friends again – but for how long? Tom and Jerry have one of the most celebrated love-hate relationship in the history of the cinema, extending even into the concert hall (*below*).

If cats really were impossible to train, as many people – usually not cat owners – tend to think, they would be impossible to live with. But certainly they respond less well to any training not specifically in their own interests than many other domesticated animals.

Unlike many dogs, cats on the whole dislike performing. They distrust laughter, always suspecting that they are being laughed *at*, whereas a dog will join in and possibly prance around to get more applause. Cats are harder to reward, because of their suspicion of strange food and the difficulty of feeding them from the hand, and they preserve a distance when they choose to, quite unlike the more heavily dependent dog. For all these reasons, it has – with benefit to cats in general – historically been less possible to make the cat the servant of man than the dog.

All this affects any owner who tries to photograph his cat. The development of fast film and fast cameras has been a blessing in this respect, but any serious photography of cats, unless you accidentally catch them in action, involves a good deal of time and a large number of (often wasted) exposures.

## Cartoon cats

This may explain why cats have played a relatively minor part in show business. No real cat has achieved the super-stardom of, say, Rin-Tin-Tin or Lassie. (With cartoon cats, of course, it's a different story, with Felix,

Fritz and Tom of *Tom and Jerry* fame all making their mark in films.) A handful of films have offered cats leading parts, such as *Rhubarb*, featuring a cat of that name, and *That Darn Cat!* in which a cat never called anything else inadvertently helps to trail bank robbers. But felines in films are more often mere walk-ons, though they can be used with great dramatic effect. A notable example is in *The Third Man*, when Joseph Cotton, making a rendezvous in Vienna with the elusive Harry Lime, played by Orson Welles, notices a kitten stalking the street, and watches it stop to investigate something. The camera swings slowly up, and we see that it is sniffing the feet of Harry Lime, concealed in the shadows.

On television, there was, of course, Morris of NBC's *Today* program, and older viewers will remember Pyewacket in *Bewitched*, but cats' TV appearances have been mainly in advertising. One British carpet manufacturer based its whole brand image for decades on a sparkling silvery chinchilla as a symbol of comfort, to such an extent that the British often refer to chinchillas as Kosset cats. There have been a number of Kosset cats over the years – always the same breed, however – and the last incumbent was a cat called Solomon, who also had film experience with walk-ons in *Diamonds are Forever* and *A Clockwork Orange*. But is it significant that when cats are shown in cat food advertising, they are usually at the mundane business of feeding, when it is easier to film them.

*Above and below:* If you're a cat, it's absolutely no trouble advertising carpets. All this well-known chinchilla has to do is to sit around looking beautiful – and that's no trouble either.

*Left:* One of the best-loved children's fixtures on British TV is the magazine program *Blue Peter.* The tabbies Jack and Jill, seen here, are only two of the pets that regularly appear on it.

# Showing cats American style

In the United States, as in most places outside Britain and some British Commonwealth countries, show cats are generally judged publicly in the ring, being transferred to ring pens as each class is announced. The pens in the body of the hall where the cats spend most of their day are not seen by the judges, so they may be deco-rated with photographs, rosettes and ribbons recalling past triumphs, and may also carry the name and address of the owner or breeder. (One of the smaller US associations, however, the American Cat Council, has held British-style shows.)

Many shows in the United States are two-day affairs,

so it is necessary to arrange accommodation for both cat and owner, and to take a two-day supply of the cat's usual food. Show time is no time to be forced to try out new items of diet. You will also need a travelling basket or equivalent, bed and bedding, litter tray, food and water bowls (the last three items for the pen as well as for

use away from the show), and a blanket for the pen. Remember to have got your cat used to the blanket, or a similar one, as part of its general show training. It should go without saying that, whatever expense and trouble you have gone to, you should not take your cat to the show if it is at all sickly.

## Moment of truth

Procedure for transferring cats from their hall pens to the judging ring pens varies. At some shows, they are taken by the judges' stewards, but in others it is up to the owners to take them. So it is vital to find out what happens at any particular show, and if the job is left to the owner it is important to keep an ear cocked for the public address announcement of your particular class. From the ring cages, the stewards will bring each cat to the judges' table in turn, and your heart will be in your mouth as the result of months, perhaps years, of your work is critically examined. There is nothing you can do now, however, except keep your fingers crossed.

Although the ring judging procedure is almost universal in the United States, the method of awarding points is not. The Cat Fanciers' Association, the largest cat organization in the States and indeed in the world, awards points on a feature-by-feature basis, the importance attached to different features varying from breed to breed. Other associations, though they may publish guidelines on the proportions of points given for different features, rely more on overall assessment of the cat.

## Judging standards

These complexities and differences make it necessary for anyone going in for showing cats to obtain and study the judging rules – "the standards" – of the association of their choice. It is good to do this for all the associations operating in a given area, in any case, as even quite a modest local show will be advertised as being judged according to the standards of this or that association. Note also that pedigree cats must be registered with the association organizing the show at which they are to be exhibited.

If you are new to showing, your cat will probably make its debut at a small local show, and this is a good way for both cat and owner to gain experience. Many of the finer points of successful showing can be learned only by listening and observing, exchanging tips with other owners, and studying the competition. Your cat's showmanship will also benefit from the experience of being penned and handled, and especially from the critical handling of the judges.

*Left:* Comfortable in her cradle, a prize-winning calico Persian takes in her decorated surroundings.

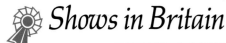

British cat shows differ from those in the United States and many other countries in one important way: the judges perambulate between the show pens, using a trolley as a judges' table, and judge the cats then and there. The public, including the owners, are excluded while the major part of the judging is completed. The show pens are plain and unadorned, to avoid influencing judgement, and any razzmatazz is left to the section of the show given over to commercial stands.

Shows are held for one day only because of the shorter distances involved – though this makes it a very long day for the more distant exhibitors. (Quarantine regulations in Britain, designed to maintain the country's nearly 80-year rabies-free record, prevent American or other non-resident owners from exhibiting there.)

### Basic equipment

Essential equipment for a British show includes a plain white woven blanket (cellular weaves and ribbon binding are prohibited), a water-bowl, a litter tray and food bowl of white plastic, and a white elastic collar to carry the number disc. Cats must arrive in a travelling basket or carrier; they may not be brought on a leash or carried in the arms. The cat's vaccination certificate, show documentation, last-minute grooming requirements, cat litter and food will also be needed.

In Britain, all the cats are "vetted in" – that is, given a veterinary examination. If there are any signs of parasites, diarrhea, skin disease, ear mites, symptoms of nose or eye infection, or pregnancy, your cat will not be permitted to enter. Once vetted in, you take your cat to the appropriate numbered pen, which you are allowed to disinfect if you wish, using a safe disinfectant (see pages 170-1).

### Preparing the pen

Ensure that the white blanket is comfortable and neatly arranged, and that there is water in the bowl and litter in the litter tray. You may feed the cat (though some owners do not recommend it) but, if you do, the bowl must be removed before the judging starts. Any necessary last-minute grooming should be only of the "last lick" variety. Remember that if you are tense and fussy this will be communicated to the cat and perhaps prevent it from doing its best. An everyday, matter-of-fact approach is good. Below the pen there will be a curtained area where you can leave your grooming equipment, the food-bowl, and any other odds and ends during the judging.

Judging normally takes about two hours at a large show, and during that time you will have to contain your patience and share notes with your fellow-exhibitors. This is a good opportunity to look around the commercial section to see if there are any new ideas or gadgets of interest.

*Left:* Judging at a British show. The judges visit each cat in turn. After being judged, this big Colorpoint Longhair will go back into the plain pen in which he is spending the rest of the day.

*Right:* Rosettes from shows past and present surround this superb Turkish Van in its moment of glory.

## Signs of success

After the judging, you may display on the pen any rosettes, ribbons or judges' cards, and when all the judging (including "Best of Show") has been completed you may, if you wish, seek out the appropriate judge to discuss your own entry. The judge will have made comments on each entry in the judging book, and may be prepared to tell you what these are. But it is understandable if, after a tiring day expending a great deal of critical energy, a judge declines to talk, and there is no obligation to do so. Most, however, will.

You will be expected to leave your cat, winner or not, in its pen until the show closes to the public. Remember that shows are organized for the pleasure of the general cat-loving public as well as for the owners of show cats, and most shows rely financially on the entrance money paid by those who have come to look rather than exhibit. In any case, you can use the time profitably by seeking out the prizewinners – especially those in the same breed class – and noting points. Finally, when the public has gone, transfer your cat to its travelling container, dispose of water and cat litter, whether used or not, and leave the pen clean.

There is obviously some risk of cross-infection when a large number of cats are brought together, though less in Britain where they remain in the same pen for the duration of the show. Keep a close eye on your cat for a few days to catch any early warning signs of infection, parasites, or digestive problems. Sometimes you will have to miss a show.

*Above:* Grand Premier Shirar Tom Thumb. As his title implies, this British cat is a neuter.

*Right:* To be a winner, you don't always need a pedigree as long as your tail. Cats can be entered for special non-pedigree classes as well. One non-pedigree winner at the National was this aptly-named "Tapestry Charm".

*Left:* Top cat Grand Champion Miramar Pakeha. This silver-tipped British Shorthair is one of the recent stars of the largest cat show in the world: the National Cat Club Show of Britain, held every winter in London.

# 6 SURVIVAL IN THE WILD

Except for the domestication of *Felis lybica*, and limited use of the cheetah and the caracal as hunting animals, man's relationship with the wild cats native to areas where he has settled has not been a particularly happy one. Cats have preyed too often upon his stock animals, and have competed for prey, such as rabbits, hares and even deer. Typically, the cats have retreated to the wildest and least accessible parts of the country. An example is the history of the European wild cat (*F. silvestris*) in Scotland. Once widely distributed throughout the country, it has been steadily driven back by farming and urban development until it is now found only in the northernmost areas of Europe, in undisturbed mountainous habitats.

A few species, however, have been relatively undeterred by man's presence, and one of these is the bay lynx or bobcat (*F. rufus*) of North America. This is found across a wide band of North and Central America stretching from sub-Arctic Canada to central Mexico. Its natural habitat is dry scrubland, where it lies concealed among vegetation by day, helped by its barred and spotted coat. It hunts at night, taking on fairly large prey such as hares, rabbits and the occasional young deer.

As winter comes on, it becomes increasingly desperate for food and increasingly wide-ranging in its tastes, and at this stage it is confident enough to approach the outskirts of towns and cities, where it feeds on the suburban rat population. This ability to adapt its diet to severe conditions – it will even turn to carrion if there is nothing else, and will also take fish and frogs – is most probably the key to the continuing survival and wide distribution of the lynx.

Water may not be to all cats' liking, but it's a habitat like any other – and there's plenty of food to catch. This Cape Wild Cat, though, is heading for dry land.

It is significant that there are few members of the genus *Felis* on the list of endangered species. Of the six *Panthera*, two – the tiger and the snow leopard – are listed as endangered in the "Red Data Book" of the International Union for the Conservation of Nature, while the clouded leopard is also under threat, though to a lesser extent. One species and subspecies of the thirty or so species of *Felis* are also on the endangered red list: the ocelot (*F. pardalis*) and Spanish lynx (*F. lynx pardina*).

Generally, members of the *Felis* species are resilient survivors because of their ability to adapt as the environment changes around them. For example, one of the most common Asiatic cats, the leopard cat (*F. bengalensis*), is, as its spotted coat suggests, a natural forest-dweller. But with the decline of forests in its distribution area it has adapted to life in the scrubland. Here, no doubt it has to work harder for its living, since scrub will give it less cover and so make it more easily avoided by potential prey species; but it has suffered no apparent decline in numbers.

## Felis the adaptable

Other forest-dwelling cats, far from being driven out by the approach of civilization, have moved up to exploit it. Like the bobcat in North America, the jungle cat (*F. chaus*), which is one of the domestic cat's possible marginal ancestors (see pages 12-13), will approach human settlements in search of food. It may well be that the smaller the cat, the better its ability to adapt.

Significantly, the Spanish lynx *F. lynx pardina* is the only *Felis* species outside the Americas to be under threat, and it is the third largest of the small cats, with an average weight around 40 to 45 lb (18-20 kg). It inhabits only the remote interior uplands of Spain and Portugal,

and in 1970 there were no more than 200 individuals remaining in the wild.

A particularly interesting question for the future is posed by the numerous small cats of the South American forests, now under intensive clearance. These great stretches of forest are home for an amazing variety of *Felis* species, nine in all, ranging from the puma (*F. concolor*), through the margay or tree ocelot (*F. wiedii*) to the smallest of the forest cats, the tiger cat (*F. tigrina*), which weighs only about 6 lb (2.7 kg) on average, and the similarly-sized Geoffroy's cat (*F. geoffroyi*), named after the nineteenth-century French naturalist Etienne Geoffroy Saint-Hilaire.

## Forest to scrub

Geoffroy's cat and the pampas cat (*F. colocolo*), which, despite its common name, is a natural forest-dweller, have already moved out to the scrublands and grasslands, and it is likely that, as the forests shrink, more species will have to do so, with greater or less success. It may be that one or other of them will be so successful in adaptation that it will rival the record of the African wild cat (*F. lybica*), not, however, a forest cat, which has so triumphantly colonized southern Europe, northern Africa and Asia by its willingness to exploit the potential of almost every kind of habitat, not excluding that provided by humans.

*Right:* Above the snowline, a Lynx carries off its prey to a spot where it can eat undisturbed and in safety: an instinct that lies at the root of the domestic cat's habit of bringing prey home.

*Left and far left:* Lookalikes. Many of the smaller members of the cat family look very similar, with their spots, stripes, blotches and slightly rounded tips to their ears. The cat on the far left is a young Margay or Tree Ocelot from South America. Its more densely-patterned neighbor is a Geoffroy's Cat, also from South America.

Forest cats are distinguished by their spotted or dappled coats, which camouflage them as they lie in wait for prey. The cats of the deserts, mountains and plains similarly use their light colored coats as camouflage to blend with their rocky, sandy or grassy habitats.

These cats are smaller in general than the forest-dwellers, and those that do not need great climbing skills, such as the sand cat (*F. margarita*) of the North African and Middle Eastern deserts, have rather stumpy legs, giving them a low-slung appearance. The sand cat weighs on average only about 5 lb (2.3 kg), and its distinguishing feature is the growth of generous coverings of hair over the paws, which may well be a device as insulation against the desert heat. A desert cat must be able to withstand cold nights as well as the heat of the day, and clearly a nocturnal animal, moving about when the temperature is at its lowest and quiescent when the sun is up, is well-adapted to such a habitat.

Another relatively short-legged small cat is the manul (*F. manul*) or Pallas's cat, a medium-weight 9 lb (4 kg) cat found in the deserts and steppes of the USSR, Afghanistan, Baluchistan, Kashmir, Tibet and western China. The alternative common name, incidentally, commemorates one of the great pioneers of natural history exploration. Peter Pallas was a German who, after studying medicine, turned to natural history and was appointed in 1768 to the Imperial Academy of Science in St Petersburg (now Leningrad). It was on an expedition across southern Asia to China in the following year that he identified the species now associated with his name.

## Historical relationship

The largest of the non-forest-dwellers is the caracal (*F. caracal*), found in Africa and south-west Asia. Weighing up to 50 lb (22.7 kg), it has the characteristic short tail and tufted ears of the lynx group, and indeed its alternative common names are caracal lynx or Persian lynx. Its size enables it to take on a wide range of prey from gazelles and small deer down to hares and peafowl, and it is one of the few wild cats which has had a historical relationship with man, having, in India, been tamed and trained as a hunter.

As a group, the cats of the deserts, mountains and plains seem to be fairly secure. They pose little threat to man or his livestock (unlike, for example, the puma, whose depredations on the pioneers' stock was the main reason for its decline in North America), and, of course, the African wild cat has so far cemented its relationship with man as to form part of the zoological tree of the domestic cat.

*Left:* A European Wild Cat gapes in a luxurious yawn. A big tabby with pronounced stripes, this species probably contributed to the make-up of the domestic cat.

*Below:* Biggest of the small cats, a Puma basks in the sun.

*Right:* The Manul or Pallas's Cat, another possible – though unlikely – contributor to the domestic cat's genetic make-up. An inhabitant of the steppes of Central Asia, it can hoot like an owl and yelp like a dog.

# Water habits

Almost all cats, large and small, unite in their dislike of water, though many desert-dwellers tend to live close to rivers and streams so that they can pick off the prey that come to drink. Even in desperation, however, few species would actually enter the water in search of food, although, if necessary, most cats can swim.

However, apart from the behavior of the domestic Turkish Van (see page 90), there are a few notable exceptions. The tiger is one, for it will often sit or lie in shallow water to cool off in very hot weather. It is a strong swimmer, and will readily enter water in pursuit of prey. Tigers have been seen to catch turtles and fish, and even to swim out to larger prey stranded on islands cut off by rising flood waters. But there is no knowing, of course, that other cat species, with their instinct for survival and their long record of success, would not perform similar acts if they were forced to.

## Webbed paws

Among small cats, there are two which get at least part of their living from the water. The fishing cat (*F. viverrina*) which lives in the swamplands of south-east Asia is not idly named. Indeed, its paws are slightly webbed and its claws do not retract fully, suggesting that the claws are frequently needed to grip muddy banks as it returns from the water to eat its catch, while the webbed paws aid swimming.

Given the predilection of cats for fish, it is perhaps surprising that more species have not adapted themselves to plunder the abundant food available in fresh water habitats. But another one that has is the serval (*F. serval*), a handsome, spotted, long-legged and large-eared creature that inhabits a broad band across Africa south of the Sahara and north of the Kalahari. Its range of prey is unusually wide, extending from lizards and large insects at one extreme to the burrowing mole-rat at the other. Its skills include swimming, and it never strays far from water.

*Right:* Feline reflections. This tiger looks as at home in the water as it would on dry land. Under the surface, its big paws are acting as powerful paddles, thrusting it along. The tail still has a steering function. Tigers have been known to catch turtles; their much smaller cousin (inset) is content with a fish from someone's garden pool.

It is night in the inner city. The theater crowds have long since gone home, and even the late late bars and clubs are closed and dark. Lighted shop windows display their merchandise to the empty sidewalks. In silent offices, typewriters are covered and inert. The early hours are the quietest hours.

Yet all is not still. On patches of waste ground, in the alleyways between buildings, at the fringes of parking lots and in factory yards, there is stealthy movement. The city's population of feral cats is up and about its nocturnal business.

Feral cats – descended from escaped domesticated cats – are, in a sense, the down-and-outs of the feline world, but they do better for themselves than their human counterparts. They remind us that, unlike the dog, *F. catus* has never allowed itself to be so assimilated into the world of humans that it can no longer fend for itself. The feral cat lives in a world of its own, poised between true wildness and true domesticity; it retains, like all domestic cats, some of the characteristics of its truly wild cousins while, at the same time, displaying some affinity, perhaps based on a sort of folk memory, with human beings.

## Feral matriarchies

Some feral cats live entirely without human intervention or contact, and these, unusually for cats, gather in colonies based on a matriarchy; the only other cats to live collectively are lions. But, in fact, most feral cats rely on – or at any rate enjoy – human support from the kindly old lady who feeds them each evening, the factory workers who bring cat food in with them every day, or the security guard who welcomes their company at night and shares his supper with them. There are also rich pickings from what man has left uneaten in the garbage cans outside restaurants and hamburger joints. Many, in return, provide mouse- and rat-catching services, dividing the city between them into territories. They breed copiously, occasionally adding to their number and the strength of their stock from among domestic strays and lost or dumped queens.

*Left:* A colony of city cats groom themselves, meditate and socialise in the slanting sun of a Roman evening.

*Below:* Apart from the domestic cat, lions are the only felines to whom living in groups comes naturally.

Off the north-west coast of Scotland, on the edge of the Atlantic, are the Hebrides, a group of about 500 islands, most of which are uninhabited. One of these is Shillay, which until 1942 had a small human settlement consisting of the families of the lighthouse-keepers and a few lobster fishermen. In 1942 the lighthouse was closed, and the families moved away to the nearby larger island of North Uist, leaving behind their cats. The cats thrived, interbred, and formed a feral colony. Their descendants now lead completely feral lives and have human contact for only a few weeks in the summer when lobstermen camp on the island.

The feral cats of Shillay are representatives of one extreme of feral life, almost completely isolated from man and thoroughly independent of his support. No new breeding lines come in from outside the colony, and with each generation the tight social bonds are strengthened. The colony's isolation, though it might lead to weakening through excessive interbreeding, affords protection against infectious diseases.

For the other extreme, we might take an abandoned factory site where the former semi-feral factory cats have stayed on to form a colony. Even when the factory was occupied they will have had more closely-knit social lives, based on the territories of the queens and the larger ones of the toms, than any group of neighboring domestic cats. The departure of the human workforce, giving freedom for the cats to colonize the factory buildings, will have led to some rearrangement of territories and possibly some infilling and strengthening of the breeding stock by newly-arrived "squatters".

Alternatively, some remnants of the old factory life may linger on; former workers who live nearby may still come in daily with food. Later, a new company may move in and start up the factory again, in which case the feral cats will loosen their hold on wildness and join the new factory family, provided that the interval is not so great that the tribal memory is lost. "Take it or leave it" is the basis of this colony's relationship with humans.

## Catacombs

Between these two extremes lies a whole range of situations in which more or less feral cats live in some kind of relationship, or none, with humans. There are countless permutations. Typical environments are dockyards, quaysides, armed forces establishments, hospitals and other institutions, garbage dumps, schools and colleges with extensive grounds – anywhere where there may be a chance of food for free (that is, without the labor of hunting and killing it) or, alternatively, where (as on garbage tips) prey species are plentiful. An added bonus in winter, as for example in the basement catacombs of office blocks and hospitals, is warmth from heating ducts and hot water pipes.

A place where the queens of the colony may retire to give birth is an added attraction, and they will make full use of any large bins, cardboard or wooden boxes, packing-cases, stacks of lumber and out-of-the-way enclosures. One abandoned steelworks had a series of lean-to shacks at intervals along the outside walls of the rolling shop where the men could go for a smoke and a "wet" during their breaks. After the factory closed, and before it was demolished, these shacks, with their bits of old matting, discarded lunch-boxes and so on became favorite kittening-boxes for the feral queens.

### Ferals on farms

Feral cats, although more obvious to the city dweller, are not an urban phenomenon. The rural version typically inhabits a ruined farm or a set of remote outbuildings.

The farm cat, now less prized for its rat-catching abilities than in earlier times when there was more on-farm storage of corn, occupies a position halfway between the feral and the truly domestic cat. Much of its time may be spent in circumstances similar to the feral; but on a dairy farm, for example, it is likely to hang about hopefully at milking-time, and it will also appear on cue if anything going on in the farm buildings, such as the moving of straw bales, seems likely to promise good hunting.

*Above:* Three feral cats happily sunning themselves on the outskirts of Bankok in Thailand.

*Right:* Feral cats often do well out of hand-outs from kindly human residents on their patch. These are in Tunisia.

Inevitably, less is known in detail about the lifestyle of the feral cat than about that of its domestic relative. The domestic cat leads a more easily observable life and comes to be known and understood intimately by its owner. Much of the life of the feral is, and will remain, hidden. But studies which have been made, particularly in the United States, Britain, Australia and Scandinavia, give us some information about the wild life.

As early as the 1930s, McMurry and Sperry were studying feral cats in Oklahoma, and among other important studies was one carried out by Hubbs in the 1940s in Sacramento Valley, California. In the 1970s studies of feral cats in Tasmania and New South Wales, Australia, were published, and in Britain Tabor, Dards and others conducted a series of detailed investigations of specific feral cat colonies. There is, across the world, quite a network of students of feral cats who are continually probing the mysterious half-world where cat meets man as a fellow-partner in the same environment.

## Ferocious ferals

Along with the giant hogweed and the super-rat, the giant feral cat is becoming a familiar figure in urban mythology, especially when the papers run short of news. The *Sydney Morning Herald* reported in 1971 that the wildlife of interior Australia was being decimated by giant cats weighing up to 25 lb (11.3 kg), roughly double that of a large domestic cat. There were no indigenous domestic cat ancestors in Australia, so these monsters must have been bred up from imported progenitors, if they existed at all. No more was heard, so presumably the human inhabitants of central Australia sleep safely in their beds. In fact, far from growing fat on the spoils of freedom, most feral cats, male or female, tend to be very slightly smaller and lighter than their typical domestic counterparts, from which it may be concluded that, whatever the papers may say, it's no fun being feral.

*Above:* The price of victory. The fringed ear of a feral tom, with his typically heavy cheeks, is a legacy of battles over territory and females.

*Left:* Feral cats in a city square collect round the food regularly provided for them by well-wishers. The ones sitting furthest out from the center have probably already eaten their fill.

*Right:* Nursery, climbing-frame and home: for these feral kittens, a hollow log can serve all purposes. If they are to survive, they will need their mother's training and all their wits about them.

Clearly, the feral cat lives a more risky life than the cherished domestic cat which is probably brought in at night, has someone to check on its movements and, if necessary, help it out of tight corners. An entire tom in particular is more likely to wander into hostile territory and suffer the consequences. An outbreak of disease in a feral colony may spread unchecked, whereas the domestic cat will be cared for by a vet.

Where feral cats lose out most of all is in their greater exposure to injury from traffic, falls, accidental poisoning and all the other hazards of a semi-wild life, together with the lack of support that a domestic cat receives under such circumstances. They are also vulnerable to the attentions of mindless louts with air-rifles, shotguns, or even, in the United States, hand-guns.

## Garbage food

In view of the well-known tendency of fully domesticated cats to turn up their noses at unfamiliar food, it is surprising how their tastes broaden under the threat of starvation, if they go feral. A study in Pennsylvania in 1954 showed that the food of urban feral cats consisted of about 85 per cent garbage and 15 per cent rodents and birds. In the country, these proportions were roughly reversed.

Either way, the food has to be found, which is not the case with the domestic cat. But studies in Britain have shown that if there are elderly ladies prepared to act as auxiliary feeders to feral colonies, the cats will happily turn to them. Cats, it seems, are always ready to be accepted back, at least partially, into the human fold.

*Above:* This feral spotted tabby kitten looks strikingly like his mother, and is not much smaller. But that doesn't mean he would turn down a free drink if it's on offer!

*Left:* Yes – or no? The relationship between these two ferals hangs balanced on a knife-edge: they may accept each other, or they may not. The pictures on this and the opposite page were taken by biologist and cat specialist Roger Tabor in the UK.

The common image of a feral cat colony is one of constant fighting and bickering over territory and mates. In fact, the level of aggression is higher among domestic cats competing for the limited territories of the suburbs than it is among the wider-ranging ferals. Squabbles among domestic cats usually happen when they meet accidentally, perhaps as a newcomer stakes out a territory or when, by some misreading of the light, cats which normally patrol at different times happen to be about at the same moment.

Domestic cats, it must be remembered, are relative strangers to each other, spending more time indoors than out. Though their relationships when they are outside can be related to "natural" ones, they are nevertheless dominated by the domestic side of their lives. Feral cats, by contrast, inhabit a world whose rules and customs are entirely known to members of the group. With patience, human watchers have learnt something about them, too.

A particular feature of colony life is "companionship at a distance". After the kitten stage has passed, cats do not sit together, but they maintain a relationship by sitting at a distance which depends on the amount of space available. A similar pattern of behavior can be seen in people taking their places in a restaurant where they can choose where they sit. When the restaurant first opens and business is quiet, tables will be filled in a scattered fashion, even if the customers know each other by sight, as happens in restaurants near office blocks. Only under the pressure of numbers are people prepared to sit more closely together.

## Maps and information

The common "language" of a feral cat colony is established by scent. The pads of a cat's paws deposit scent, and so the paths taken by different cats enable each to build up a "scent map" of its territory. At the same time, the rubbing of the coat against doorways, posts, and sometimes even particular tufts of grass leaves behind information for other passing cats and also, it has been suggested, collects information which the cat later interprets when it washes its coat.

The entry of a stranger into the tightly-knit community of a feral cat colony is by no means impossible, and indeed the admission of stray queens is the means by which a colony's breeding line is strengthened; but acceptance of a newcomer is a slow process. Typically, an intruder will approach too confidently and be "seen off", when it will retire to the boundary and observe events. It will then make more cautious approaches, interspersed with long, relaxed periods of "companionship at a distance".

An entire tom will have to win a place after a fight, but, provided the site and the food supply are not restricted and no liberties are taken in competition for food, a queen or a neuter will slowly gain acceptance and add its own scent to the colony language.

*Below:* "Companionship at a distance" seen on the streets. The upright tails signify a friendly greeting.

In an area – say, in the suburbs – where domestic cats are allowed out, they will neatly carve up the available gardens, public grass areas, pathways and roads into separate territories where the only conflicts that arise are likely to be on the boundaries, so long as no newcomer arrives. The mistake is often made of thinking of cats' territories as rather like the walls of a city of the ancient world, which the cats patrol in order to defend. It seems more likely, however, that the boundaries are defined not by scent-markings along them but by markings at separate points, which are the ends of tracks leading from the cat's home base.

Male cats range farther than female, in the hope of finding more available females to mate with, and in the suburban pattern their territories will include a number – perhaps half a dozen or more – female territories.

The territorial structure among feral cats is more complex. An urban feral site will include a number of places where food is likely to be found – the garbage bay, for example, or perhaps the place where a kindly human being turns up each evening with canned food. Ferals cannot afford the domestic cat's luxury of separate and distinct territories. So the territories of the females, and the larger ones of the males, overlap, centering on the feeding points. In rural areas, the territories of both males and females are proportionately larger and may include a larger number of feeding points such as individual barns, the dairy, isolated cottages with garbage left outside, and so on. A night-visiting tom may well, in the country, patrol an area of one square mile or more.

## Country scavengers

Feral cats tend to be tolerated more in the country than in the city, perhaps because of the residual feeling that anything that helps to keep down the rodent population is a good thing. In fact, the introduction of combine harvesters and enclosed grain silos has, by itself, drastically reduced the rural rat population, while the spread of urbanization towards the countryside often means that rural ferals can eat more easily by scavenging than by hunting. But in any case, the country-dweller has more important things to worry about – such as the depredations of foxes and other wild life – than the occasional feral cat.

In the city, there are attempts from time to time to reduce or eradicate feral cat colonies (see pages 134-9), notably by hospital authorities worried about hygiene. There have been a number of successful schemes where feral cats have been neutered and returned to their colonies, new arrivals being discouraged by controlling garbage disposal and restricting or forbidding auxiliary feeding. It has been suggested that this, rather than mere clearance of a colony, is the more useful course of action, since if the cats were simply removed they would be replaced within a short time by a new group. This process would, in turn, be partly arrested if the continual traffic of stray and dumped cats into the feral world could be halted. Certainly, at least part of the problem of urban ferals begins with the laziness or ignorance of owners of pet females who do not have them spayed.

*Right:* Not the smartest area of the city, but there are good pickings here for a resident feline. There could be some tasty meals in the garbage – and possibly mice as well.

*Left:* A big tabby hurries off with its kill, a full-grown rabbit, evidence of both its strength and of its skill as a hunter. Living off the land presents it with few problems.

It is widely believed, even among experienced cat-owners, that because cats appear to be so self-sufficient it is no great disaster if they stray because they can always fend for themselves.

Sadly, this is simply not true. Although in nature the cat's survival instinct is strong, often the effect of domestication is to blunt this instinct and turn it in the direction of its host home and family. A cat living in a house full of young children, for example, will use its survival instinct to preserve its privacy – but at the expense of skills which would enable it to survive outside as a stray.

The two groups of potential strays most at risk are Siamese, with their sensitivity to cold, and all longhairs, which depend on human help with caring for their coats. An ungroomed longhair's coat would soon become matted and a haven for parasites, while self-grooming would produce hairballs. The best chance of survival for strays is among the tough domestic shorthairs, especially if they have had previous experience as strays. But all cats are vulnerable away from their home range. In Baltimore, for example, about 5000 cats die on the roads each year, while mortality rates in many other towns are not counted.

## Condemned to death

Declawed cats stand no chance at all in the wild. They cannot hunt, they cannot defend themselves, and they are effectively condemned to death.

In North America (sometimes because of local regulations) cat-owners favor keeping their cats indoors more than in, say, Britain, but it should not be assumed that, because an owner wishes to keep his cat inside, the cat is necessarily going to respect his wishes. A day in the life of the average household provides innumerable opportunities for even a mildly curious, let alone a determined, cat to escape: the comings and goings of children, delivery calls, visits from friends, and so on. Jealousy following the arrival of a new baby or a new pet might provide a cue to stray, so particular attention should be paid at these times to avoid straying opportunities.

*Below:* Knowing the ropes. Docks, dockyards and harbors all form ideal habitats for ferals. Even if no-one feeds them, there is still plenty of food to be found.

*Right:* This beautiful feline family have found a happy home at last. Their owner rescued them from a field, and they now show no sign of their ordeal as rough-living strays.

Neutered or spayed cats have less tendency to stray. Certainly in the town, cats allowed out should be collared (use a collar with an elastic insert so that, in emergency, the cat can twist itself free) with a weatherproof, durable label giving a phone number. It is useful, too, to offer a reward. Regular routines, including feeding-times, will help a cat to measure its day and its distance from the home base.

Some cats are attracted by the interiors of vans and the warm darkness of engine compartments, and if your cat is known to be one of these care should be taken to check any visiting vehicles before they leave.

## Missing!
What if, despite all these precautions, your cat does disappear? First check that it has actually left the house. Cats, especially pregnant queens, are partial to dark corners, and yours may have taken the chance to investigate some attractive but normally forbidden area such as the linen closet. Determined and persistent calling is the obvious next step, and some strong-smelling food like sardines or tuna fish might lure a wanderer to return. In summer, or even on warm winter nights, a cat that normally comes home in the evening may well decide to stop out, and a newly-arrived adult (or a newly-removed one) may want to hole up somewhere for 24 hours to think about things. But if, say, after two nights there is no sign of your cat, then you should consider calling the police and any local animal welfare organizations, animal shelters and cat clubs, veterinarians (in case of injury), and perhaps ask around among neighbors, friends, and especially local children, whose grapevine is more effective than anyone's. Remember that your cat may simply have "adopted" another family; some strays find a new home simply by force of character.

Cats first approached man on the basis of a mutually satisfactory deal: man would provide shelter and maybe some food, while the cats would help deal with one of the great threats to man's health and food supply: rodents. This is still the basis of the relationship between some feral cats and the people around them. Arable farms (though less with mechanization than formerly) and to a lesser extent stock farms, stables, breweries and food-processing plants, docks, hotels and other catering establishments, all need either resident cats or feral or semi-feral hangers-on.

The scale of the service an expert hunter can perform is indicated by the record of one female cat that patrolled London's White City sports stadium for a six-year period in the 1920s and 1930s, and notched up nearly 12 500 kills, an average of five-and-a-half rats a day. As cats tend to go for young rats – it is a brave cat that will take on a fully-grown adult, though some do – they are an effective means of population control, especially in areas where poisoning would be hazardous. From Roman times onwards, cats have also been noted as mole-catchers and so as a boon for gardeners, though the moles are not normally eaten.

Problems arise, however, when feral cats become too obvious. The noise of toms on the hunt for a mate, spraying in areas such as apartment blocks, warehouses and factories, the hazards posed by unburied feces in areas where cats are unable to exercise their instinct to cover their droppings, the presence of cat fleas, and (outside a few countries like Britain which are rabies-free) the possible spreading of rabies, are among the triggers which, from time to time, set off public protest and (usually half-hearted) control campaigns. The stage is then set for a dispute between cat welfare organizations and the would-be controllers.

## Cat control

The arguments for control would be more impressive if it could be shown that it works over the long term. The evidence is far from convincing. It was noted on pages 142-3 that neutering programs have been apparently successful, but it is a rule of nature that a given habitat will tend to fill up with as many representatives of as many species as it will support. Underpopulated feral sites, under this rule, will soon recover through imports from outside.

The problem is not, in any case, a static one. In any city, at any one time, new building is driving away resident feral colonies, while elsewhere demolition or simply the abandonment of property is opening up new habitats. Completed new buildings – multi-storey car parks, institutions, office blocks – may become potential new sites again; and so the carousel turns.

Given this constantly-changing situation, anyone who thinks that the feral cat population of any city can be satisfactorily controlled is almost certainly hopelessly optimistic. In any case, it can be argued, as it is by the British feral cat expert Roger Tabor, that feral cats, like feral pigeons, are now sufficiently established to have a right to be regarded as part of our wildlife. In more down-to-earth terms, it might be said that if any wild animals in our cities urgently need control, it is the packs of wild dogs that terrorize so many urban housing estates nowadays.

*Left:* No one owns this handsome feral – but he and the London woman who regularly feeds his colony have a working relationship based equally on food and respect.

*Right:* If it weren't for the tyres on the trolley, this could be a scene from any age and any place where the cat's skill at mousing has helped man to make a living.

# 7 ESSENTIAL CAT CARE

Every cared-for cat is a travelling cat at one time or another: going to the vet, going to the kennels, ʼoing on vacation. There is only one way to transport a cat satisfactorily over any distance, and that is in a purpose-made basket or other container.

Of all the requirements you need if you are going to keep a cat, this is the only one that is at all expensive. It is, of course, possible to spend a fortune on a fancy bed, a gold-blocked playhouse, or whatever. But cardboard boxes do just as well for these purposes – and they are expendable.

The greatest demand your cat will make on you, as with any pet worth sharing your life with, will be on your time. True, it will not be as insistent as the average dog; but you should be prepared, all the same, to give your time readily. The domestic cat has chosen to live with man not only to share his roof and the warmth of a home, but also to enjoy companionship, care and love.

*Left:* Autumn has arrived, but there is still enough sunshine left for these cats to enjoy. They also enjoy each other's company – and the fixtures in their comfortable outdoor house.

*Above:* Booking in. This new arrival at a boarding cattery is getting a routine check for any signs of ill-health. All catteries also ask for proof of immunization against FIE.

If possible, regular eating habits should be encouraged by putting out the bowl at a fixed time and removing any uneaten food after, say, an hour. Semi-moist and dry foods may, however, be left out safely if necessary. Needless to say, bowls should be washed out after each feed, and occasionally sterilized.

Pet stores offer a wide variety of cat tidbits for use as rewards in training or simply as an occasional treat. Cats vary hugely in their taste for these. Successes among items commonly on hand in the kitchen include small pieces of cheese (not too much, or bowel looseness may result), bacon rind and pieces of breakfast cereal. Some cats completely ignore any attempt to feed by hand, and others have difficulty in taking food in this way. Try resting a tidbit on the ends of the fingers and letting the cat lick it off.

Talk to any cat expert, or even to many owners of ordinary mongrels, and you will receive plenty of advice, often conflicting, about recommended diets. (For diets for kittens and pregnant or lactating queens, see pages 182-3, 186-7.) The fact is, however, that for an adult cat any one of the better canned foods contains a balance of proteins and nutrients which provides a complete diet, and all you have to do is to get the amount and (since cats are fussy) the brand and flavor right. The words "balanced", "complete" or "scientific" on the label (usually in the description of the contents) have legal significance and mean that the food supplies meet all nutritional requirements. Beware of cheap brands which may lack this assurance and may be composed largely of filler with chemical flavoring.

Cats are individualistic, and the correct amount of

food provided each day for any individual cat is largely a matter of trial and error, the guide being that an adult cat should maintain its body weight. The general guide for adult, non-pregnant, non-lactating cats is one ounce of balanced canned food per day for each pound of body weight. (To find out a cat's weight, weigh yourself on the bathroom scales with and without the cat in your arms, and work out the difference.) An active cat will tend to need slightly more food, and an elderly or inactive cat slightly less than this. Feeding twice a day, at morning and evening, is recommended. Many owners, however, like to give a more varied diet than just canned food.

## Gourmet meals

It is possible to make up tasty and nutritious meals based on raw or cooked heart, tongue or any other boned meat, boned cooked white fish, a little cooked cereal or vegetables, and so on. But you are unlikely to achieve the scientific mix of manufactured petfoods, which are based on years of research and experience, and unless you actually enjoy fiddling about in this way you might as well save your time. (And you will be very put out if, after all that effort, the cat turns up its nose at what you offer.)

Dry and semi-moist foods are cheaper than canned ones (and there may be less waste, since they keep better once put out) but they have the disadvantage that they may not be nutritionally complete. Veterinarians are generally cautious about recommending them. Dry foods should be given only if the cat is prepared to drink water, either separately or mixed with the food. Any sign of kidney problems, and these foods should be abandoned. Neutered males should in any case not be fed on dry foods exclusively as they may be prone to urinary troubles.

*Above:* Licking the saucer clean. The cat's rough tongue will help it scrape up every last vestige of food. The next thing on the program is a thorough nose-to-tail wash.

*Right:* Most cats dislike poking their muzzles into deep, bowl-shaped containers. Wide dishes like this plastic one are easier for them to eat from; they are also easy to clean.

*Left:* A tidbit for a new pet. This little boy knows the best way to reassure his big calico friend. Many cats are particularly fond of bite-sized bits of cheese.

The various types of cat bed available have already been discussed (see pages 50-1). It is vital that your cat should have a place to sleep where it feels comfortable and secure, since it may well spend most of its life there, especially as it gets older. It may, of course, opt for a place of its own choosing, but if this happens to be your own favorite armchair you may have strong alternative views on the matter.

Certainly, the more comfortable the facilities you provide specifically for the cat's use, the more likely they are to be used. Comfortable does not necessarily mean luxurious or expensive. As indicated earlier, many a cat sleeps happily in a cardboard box with a piece of old blanket or towelling to line the bottom.

Whatever the sleeping quarters, provide enough loose, warm material for the cat to "tread" it and make a nest of it. This lining should be shaken out at least once a week, and occasionally washed and thoroughly dried before replacing. Wicker baskets (which some experts do not recommend because of possible draughts) should be brushed weekly with a stiff hand-brush. The fancier kind of wicker basket with a foam plastic lining covered with fabric looks attractive, but is not really practical on two counts: it is difficult to clean satisfactorily because of the mixture of materials, and cats (especially kittens) may tear at the lining and ingest fragments of foam which could lodge in the throat.

Healthy cats are tolerant of both fairly low and fairly high temperatures, and in winter the normal ambient temperature of an occupied house will be sufficient for a cat overnight. But a radiator that is turned off at night will retain some welcome heat, as will pipes or ducts under the floor, and either may suggest a good site for sleeping quarters, with the litter tray fairly near but not too close. Siamese, however, are thought to be less resistant to cold and damp. The temperature of their quarters ideally should not fall below about 60°F (15.5°C).

## Toms outside

Entire toms, because of their noxious spraying behavior, are best kept outside in an enclosed area, and breeders will want to fit up similar quarters. Siting is critical. The area should be sheltered from cold winds, and it should be possible for the cat both to sit in the sun and to find a shady spot.

If the cat is to occupy these quarters permanently, there should be a sheltered section containing the bed and, for use in cold weather, an overhead safety heat-lamp mounted in such a position that it cannot be reached. The walls and roof of the area may be made of strong wire mesh on a sturdy wooden or metal frame, or alternatively based on the design of a weatherboarded shed with one of the longer sides replaced by mesh.

It will be easier to clean, and for you to use when you want to visit your cat, if it is over 6 ft (1.8 m) high. This will also provide ample vertical climbing space if you fit suitable shelves. A plank with a few battens nailed across it at intervals of 6 to 9 ins (15-22 cm) will give the cat much enjoyable exercise.

*Left:* Naughty – but sheer heaven from the feline point of view. Cats love warm places, and an airing cupboard is the snuggest, softest place in the house.

*Right:* The top of the boiler is another cosy spot – and the rug shows that the owner encourages the cat to be there. More traditional beds are shown below.

# Grooming

Because cats spend so much time grooming themselves, first-time owners often assume that that is the end of the matter, and indeed may have chosen a cat rather than another pet on the grounds that "they look after themselves". Yes, they do, up to a point, especially if they are shorthairs; but grooming by the owner is, in three important respects, an essential contribution to the quality of a cat's life.

First, a regular session of grooming and play helps to bond cat to owner. Second, it provides an opportunity for a general check on the condition of the coat, skin, paws, ears, eyes and nose. Third, loose hair which is brushed away during the molt will not be ingested to form hairballs in the stomach.

This section is about the general grooming that all cats should receive rather than the specialized attention given to show cats. Grooming-time should be a pleasure for both cat and owner. This is relatively easy to achieve if the cat has arrived as a kitten, when gentle handling and brushing from the early days will give confidence and form part of the play routine. The real problem is with newly-arrived adult cats and, ironically, with those strays or lost cats most in need of grooming but most likely to object to it. The best advice here is to start on a "little and often" basis and gradually, as the cat finds that grooming is not nearly as unpleasant an experience as it had expected, to extend the time and attention.

## Fleas and lice

Choose a time for grooming when the cat is relaxed and comfortable. First comb and then brush the coat, always working towards the tail and down the legs. Watch carefully for any fleas; cat fleas are fairly common, and multiply rapidly unless brought under control. If you discover fleas, seek veterinary advice on a suitable insecticide and follow the instructions to the letter. Some cats tend to react to the hiss of an aerosol, so powder is an alternative. Infestations of lice are rarer, and again the vet's advice should be sought. When grooming, keep an eye open for other skin disorders.

With longhairs, grooming takes longer and should be done every day. Before using the comb and brush, sort out any tangles or knots with the fingers. Slight damping of the matted hair sometimes makes this task easier. A longhair that goes outside may also pick up mud and other bits of debris. Ease this away with care and patience. When brushing a longhair, lift the brush sharply away from the coat at the end of each stroke so that the hairs stand out.

## Intoxicating cleaning

Ears and eyes may be cleaned gently with absorbent cotton dampened with warm water. Any obstinate stains on the coat such as tar or grease can be swabbed off with absorbent cotton moistened with rubbing alcohol, but be sure to keep this away from the eyes and mouth, and use it sparingly. Cats intoxicated by the fumes show the symptoms of human drunkenness. The fumes evaporate within a few minutes.

*Right:* Brought up to be accustomed to a regular daily session, a cat knows when it is time and will even demand to be groomed.

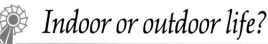

# *Indoor or outdoor life?*

The pros and cons of letting your cat have an indoor or outdoor life have already been discussed (see pages 56-7). You will quite possibly not be in a position to choose, and if circumstances dictate that your cat lives indoors you will need to make adaptations to your home.

If, for example, you have a balcony or veranda to which the cat is to have access, it must be made catproof with wire mesh. To make sure you can go in and out without setting up a cat-hunt, you may need an extra internal door. Where windows are left open, you must fix up some kind of covering frame of wire mesh, either on the same principle as a shutter or as a self-contained unit which can be slipped into place when required. Make sure that there is some place where the cat can sit or lie comfortably and observe the outside world. If the window-sill is not wide enough, extend it by screwing on an observation platform, or place an unobstructed piece of furniture close to the window.

Another requirement for the indoor cat is a supply of fresh grass, and a pot of this should be provided, well away from any house-plants. For advice on scratching-posts or pads, see pages 52-3.

*Above:* What's going on out there? Cats take very little time to learn how to use a cat-flap, and, if you allow your cat freedom to go outside, it solves a lot of problems in the home.

*Right:* Fireside domesticity, appreciated by cat and dogs alike. The Peke seems quite content to be used as a backrest by its tabby companion – but someone else is stealing most of the warmth!

*Left:* In spite of the weather, this domestic shorthair has an outdoor task that won't wait: cleaning and sharpening its claws. As the scars on the bark show, the tree is a favorite one.

## Claws and scratches

The cat's need to scratch is without doubt one of the major problems for owners of indoor cats, which can, however, be trained to use the pad or post provided rather than the furniture or carpets. The ultimate solution might seem to be declawing – the surgical removal of (usually) only the front claws. This is an unnecessary mutilation, which of course leaves the cat not only unable to climb, but also unable to defend itself if it should ever escape from the house. There are risks in the operation itself, which is, of course, irreversible. If you consider it, you must first be sure that the cat will be kept permanently indoors by you and by any subsequent owner. You also give up your chance of showing the cat at any level, because most show organizations in the United States follow the British example and outlaw declawed cats.

If, after all efforts, you really cannot train your cat to use a scratching-post or pad, the more civilized alternative to declawing is to confine the cat to an area of the house where scratches won't matter, let it go outside under close supervision, or, if it's that too much trouble, avoid keeping a cat altogether.

In some American cities, cats are allowed out of doors only on a leash. Walking on a leash does not come naturally or easily to cats, but they can be trained with patience. A harness rather than merely a collar is advised for training, and it should have elastic inserts so that it does not restrain the cat too tightly. Initially, loop a piece of string through the collar and let the cat get used to trailing this free. (Always stay with it during this.) The next stage is to hold the string lightly, and then to lead the cat. On no account pull it. When it is used to being led indoors start taking a few short excursions outside, very gradually increasing the range and scope of your outings.

A cat should never be left, even for a single night, without human attention. If you love your cat – and if you don't you shouldn't have one – this should be obvious, but the sad fact is that every year thousands of apparently well-loved family cats are turned loose to fend for themselves when their owners go on vacation.

For an overnight or weekend stay away, it may be possible to arrange for a neighbor to look in at least twice a day, but if so this must be someone the cat knows and trusts, and who is totally reliable. When you first get your cat, think about your neighbors and friends and make the initial approach before the need for a cat-sitter arises; this is not an occasion for a hit-or-miss last-minute deal.

Your sitter should know where to empty and clean the tray, how much food to give, and what kinds of games your cat likes to play. You should leave your vet's and your own phone numbers in a prominent place. Make sure that the sitter knows about the cat's night-time routine, and if you have a cat-door which you bolt at night to keep your cat in, show the sitter how it works. (Brief notes of the night-time routine, and feeding instructions, help.) Your sitter should know what words and intonations you use as a "come here" signal, and should also watch you go through your feeding, water and night routines at least once.

Unless you have very understanding or cat-loving neighbors, it is best, for longer periods of absence such as a vacation, to put your cat into boarding kennels. Kennels are very variable in the quality of environment and care they offer to their boarders, and the choice of a suitable one is something you should make well in advance. In urban areas in particular, it's as well to have two kennels on your approved list, as reservations are heavy in the vacation season and around public holidays. Your vet should be able to make recommendations. Cat-owning friends are also good sources of suggestions, advertisements in pet stores less so.

## Visit of approval

In any event, you should visit the kennels yourself before you put it on your approved list. Look not only at the state and cleanliness or otherwise of the quarters, but also at the condition and mood of the cats in residence. If they look unsettled or bored, then this place is not for you. Look around the whole premises, not merely at a few of the quarters, and try to have a chat with as many of the staff as you can. This will give you an idea of whether they are genuine cat-lovers or merely in business for the money.

Find out what certificates of vaccination are required, and whether you can bring the cat's own bed and bedding (you usually can, but it's good to check). Check also that the proprietors are insured against the death or sickness of the cats in their care. Finally, if you have been recommended to a kennels by anyone other than a vet, give your vet a call to get his opinion.

When the time comes to put your cat into kennels, make the reservation early. (It's a good idea to do it as part of your vacation planning.) Make sure that vaccination certificates will be up to date at the date of boarding. When you go along, take these with you. If yours is not the kind of cat that sleeps in a bed, a familiar rug or piece of blanket will help it feel more secure. Don't forget a toy or two.

When you check in, give your temporary address and phone number and see that it is written down. If, for example, you are touring and don't know what your movements will be, give the name and number of someone who can speak with authority in the case of illness. Agree with the kennels that a vet will be called, at your expense, if necessary, and sort out questions of liability afterwards. Finally, see your cat settled in, but don't make too much of the parting; if you are giving out distress signals, these will be infectious.

*Above:* A handsome tabby Persian greets visitors to its home-from-home from the top of its sleeping quarters. Its dirt-tray is below, beside the entrance ramp.

*Right:* A well-planned boarding cattery, with space between each individual run. Sleeping accommodation is at the back of the outdoor compartments.

If you apply the same principles to choosing a vet as you would to choosing your own physician, you won't go far wrong. Of course, in some areas you may not have much choice, but if you have moved to a district you don't know it is worth consulting with cat club secretaries and show organizers. A vet associated with a club or show is likely to be, at least to some extent, a cat enthusiast. Given the choice, a vet with a specialized small animals practice is to be preferred to an all-rounder.

But what matters in the end is not the string of letters after the vet's name, or the approval of the local cat club, so much as how well you and your cat get on with him. He should indicate sympathy with cats and their problems, and he should be able to talk to you in simple language. He should also be the kind of person you can talk to freely.

A good deal about a practice can be learned from the condition of the waiting-room and the attitude of the assisting staff. Efficiency in taking appointments and signs of good record-keeping are encouraging, but of course you will not expect appointments to run too strictly to timetable. (You, however, should always turn up on time.) It is essential to find out what the emergency out-of-hours arrangements are.

## Vaccinations

The prevalence of feline diseases varies from place to place, and the vet will advise you what vaccinations are required, and when. The most usual vaccinations are against feline infectious enteritis, respiratory virus infections ("cat flu") and, except in countries which are rabies-free, rabies. The usual age for the first vaccination is about two to three months, with annual booster jabs thereafter. You should ask the vet to combine these occasions with a general health check, which may also be wise if the cat has spent a period in boarding kennels. For veterinary attention to pregnant queens, see pages 182-3.

In the case of a newly-acquired adult cat, take the first opportunity for a general check-up with any necessary vaccinations. If you know the cat's previous owner, try to obtain its vaccination record card. If your acquisition is a stray, the vet will be able to make an estimate of its age from its weight, general condition and, in particular, the appearance of its teeth.

## Accident or illness

If you feel that the vet's attention is needed because of accident or illness (and if you suspect it, it probably is), obtain initial advice by phone. Describe the symptoms or problem as clearly as you can, and ask whether you should visit the surgery or have the vet visit you. Keep the vet's phone number with your other household emergency numbers.

The rule for all cat-owners is: "If in doubt, call in the professional". With your own illnesses, you know how you feel and so can make an informed assessment of whether you need the physician. With a cat, you can rely only on external evidence, and it is better to make an unnecessary phone call than to leave it too late.

*Left:* Going to the vet. A cat box or cat basket is a must for all cat-owners, since carrying a cat loose in a car is very dangerous. Baskets and boxes should be made of strong, claw-proof materials.

*Top right:* In the vet's surgery, a patient's ears are examined and cleaned with cotton buds.

*Bottom right:* Now a check-up for the teeth: any tartar? The vet's gentle grip also represents the first stage of giving a cat a pill: once the jaws are open, you can drop the pill into the patient's mouth. But, usually, medicating a cat is a four-handed operation!

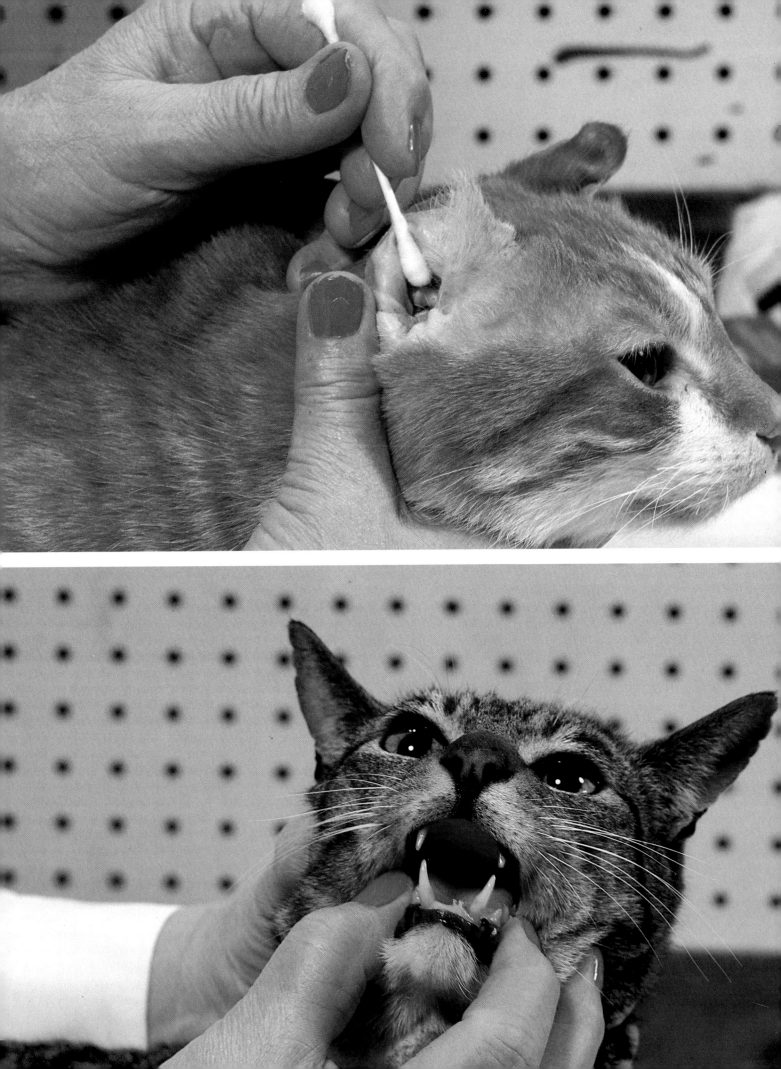

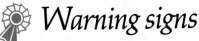 

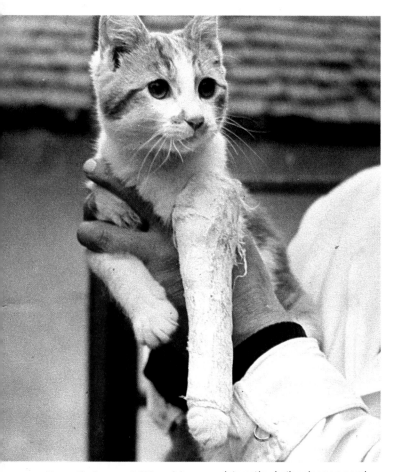

*Above:* On the mend. Although it has had its leg set in plaster, this bi-color is still taking a keen interest in what's going on around it: an important sign of its good state of health.

Let it be quite clear before this discussion of feline illnesses that most cats live completely healthy lives. They are not delicate or sickly animals by nature, and you may never have to take yours to the vet for anything more than routine check-ups and vaccinations. This is even more true if it is kept indoors all the time; preventing contact with other animals and with their feces automatically cuts out much risk of cross-infection. At the same time, you have the comfort of knowing that the sight of a sick cat is unmistakable; if anything at all is wrong, the cat looks ill.

The rule is to seek veterinary advice right away if you are worried, and even if you only need reassurance. Never attempt diagnosis yourself. In any case, if the cat is seriously ill you will need to go to the vet for medicines which may not be available from anyone else, and it is extremely difficult for the inexperienced to administer medication to cats.

Although continued *vomiting* is a warning sign, cats do vomit easily and with little apparent distress, though the noise can be appalling. An isolated instance of vomiting may simply be the result of over-eating or eating too quickly, a fur-ball, or merely the rejection of an unfamiliar food. Similarly, the occasional isolated *sneeze* is nothing to worry about; cats get dust up their noses just like humans. Nor need you rush to the vet if there is a bout of *diarrhea*, if this is the only sign of anything wrong and provided it clears up reasonably quickly. Changes in diet, or the emotional upset of, for example, a change of house, can be the cause. Persistent diarrhea, however, is a case for the vet.

## Classic symptoms

The classic symptoms of illness are: *loss of appetite, listlessness, lack of interest* in movements round about, *refusal to play,* and unusually *bad temper.* These, of course, must be related to the cat's normal behaviour. The *coat* may look dull and lifeless, and it may lie in flat, spiky segments. Some cats, when sick, *hide* themselves away in a dark corner. The appearance of the *third eyelid,* or "haw", a grayish-white membrane exending from the inside of the eye, is another sign that something could be wrong. The breathing and pulse rates (normally 30-50 and 110-140 respectively) may increase.

Cats are not prone to the vaguely unwell condition that, in humans, we call "feeling out of sorts" and their illnesses do not, unlike such human ones as the common cold, put themselves right. If you have any reason to suspect anything wrong, do not hesitate to phone the vet and ask his advice. Many cat diseases develop terrifyingly quickly, and the sooner you get help the better. Don't bother to attempt to take the cat's temperature. This is a tricky procedure at the best of times, and it will tell you very little.

*Left:* Veterinary examination, with the confident patient examining the stethoscope.

*Right:* Medicine, a tidbit, or both? Not all cats, though, are such willing patients as this.

The symbol * on these and the following pages indicates that veterinary attention and advice is essential. Do not hesitate to contact the vet.

## Abscess

*Description:* Pus-filled lump beneath the skin, caused by the entry of infection during the infliction of a cut, scratch or bite.

*Treatment:* *, antibiotic injection and/or lancing. Hot saline bathing of the abscess should be done several times daily and continued for a number of days to prevent the abscess closing too quickly and trapping the remaining pus.

## Allergies

*Description:* Adverse reactions – often gastric or a form of eczema – to certain foods, or as a result of flea-bites.

*Treatment:* Careful monitoring of diet to isolate the offending item (sometimes cow's milk or other dairy products, especially in Siamese). If this is unsuccessful, *. See also **eczema.**

## Anemia

*Description:* Loss of red blood cells which causes lack of appetite, fading of the color of the gums, and general out-of-condition appearance.

*Treatment:* *, dietary supplements, drugs or, in serious cases, blood transfusion.

## Asthma

*Description:* The constriction of airways in the lungs, causing coughing and breathing difficulties, often the manifestation of an allergy.

*Treatment:* *, followed by identification and removal of the allergen.

*Above:* Everything possible is being done for this very sick kitten, resting in its surgery basket with a downcast expression.

## Bladder infections

*Description:* Most commonly cystitis, causing frequent urination and sometimes blood in the urine. Most common in older neutered males.

*Treatment:* *, do not feed dry food.

## Bronchitis

*Description:* Inflammation of the bronchial tubes, often associated with a respiratory infection, causing coughing.

*Treatment:* *, inhalations.

## "Cat flu"

*Description:* Common name for a number of related, though different, respiratory viral infections. Some of these are very infectious, others less so, but if any respiratory viral infection is suspected it should be treated as very infectious and action (isolation from other cats, in particular) taken accordingly. Typical symptoms are eye and nose discharges, ulceration in the mouth, loss of appetite, listlessness. Two virus strains, **feline viral rhinotracheitis** and **feline calcivirus,** can be vaccinated against, but other strains occasionally appear.

*Treatment:* *, urgently if any respiratory viral infection suspected.

## Coccidiosis

*Description:* Parasitic infection of the intestines causing loose, foul-smelling motions.

*Treatment:* *, followed by scrupulous cleanliness in the litter tray.

*Left:* Although, at first sight, this red tabby does not look particularly ill, it has in fact got one of the worst cat diseases: feline leukemia virus (FeLV). Sadly, no cure has yet been found.

*Right:* A careful veterinary examination for this Siamese. One major sign that has told the owner the cat is sick is the sight of its third eyelids – or "haws" – at the inner corners of its eyes.

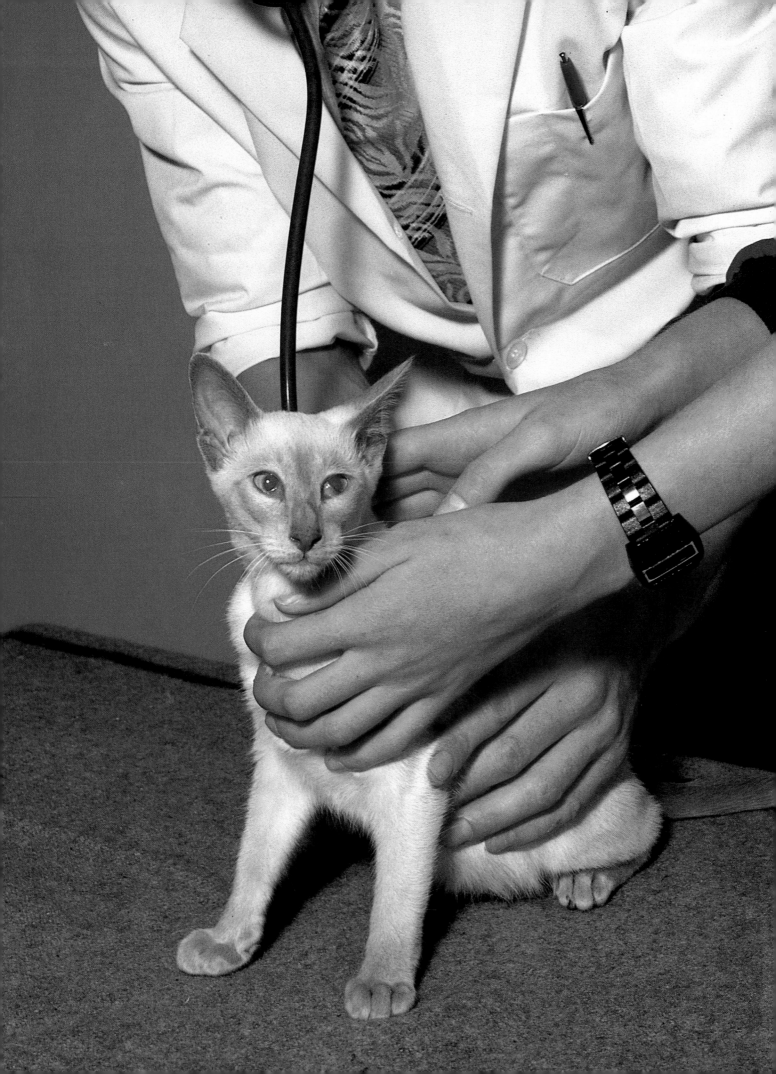

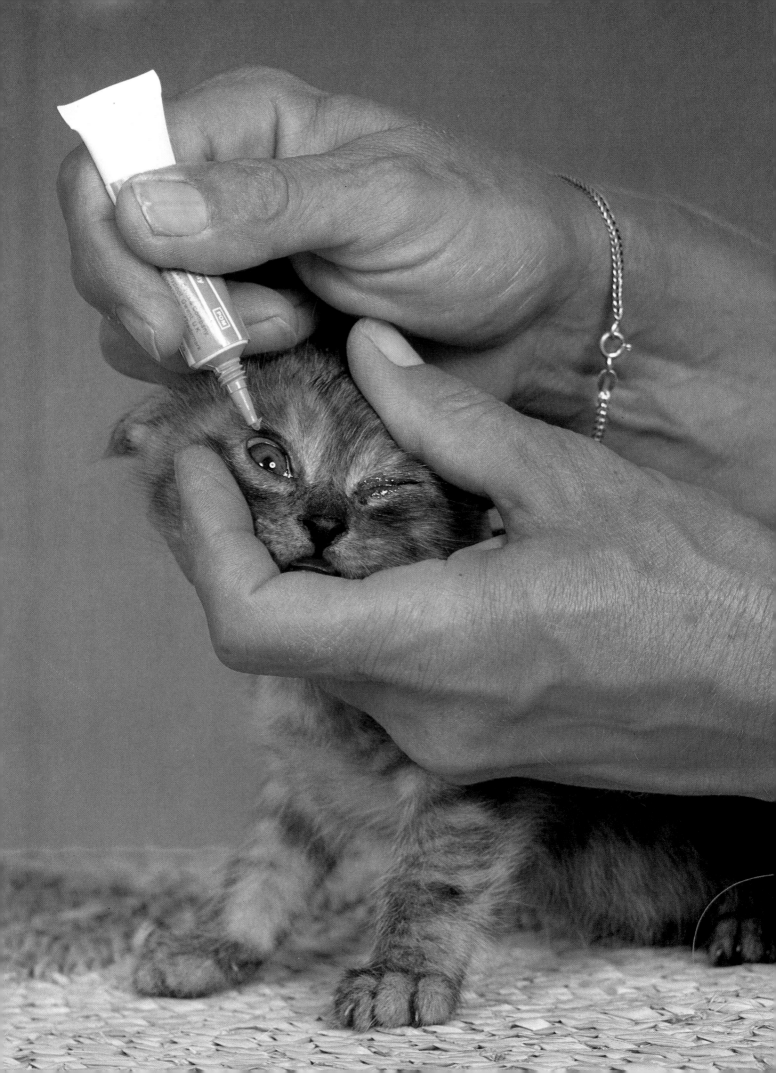

## Constipation
*Description:* Difficulty in passing motions.
*Treatment:* For an occasional attack, feed oily fish such as sardines, or merely the oil from the can, and plenty of fluids. If conditions persist, *.

## Diarrhea
*Description:* Loose and liquid motions. Feeding raw liver is a frequent cause.
*Treatment:* An occasional bout will probably clear itself. Light kaolin helps, but if condition persists for more than two days, *.

## Eczema
*Description:* Skin irritation caused by an allergy or change of diet.
*Treatment:* Prevent cat scratching by fitting a cardboard collar, de-fleaing treatment, and *.

## Feline calcivirus See "cat flu"

## Feline infectious enteritis
*Description:* Highly transmissible, rapidly-developing and usually fatal viral infection, fortunately almost 100 per cent preventable through vaccination. The symptoms are a sudden and sharp decline in health and appearance, vomiting, diarrhea and lack of interest in food and surroundings. Collapse.
*Treatment:* Phone the vet at once and tell him your suspicions. Do not take the cat to the surgery; isolate from any other cats. In unvaccinated cats, survival is extremely unlikely; but whether the cat survives or not, destroy all bedding and other items and renew. If the cat dies, do not have another for at least six months, unless previously vaccinated.

## Feline leukemia virus (FeLV)
*Description:* Malignant disease of the white blood cells which is transmissible and often causes gradual wasting, sometimes over a period of years. Symptoms and signs can be very variable.
*Treatment:* *, but the disease is usually fatal and there is no effective treatment.

## Feline viral rhinotracheitis See "cat flu"

## Jaundice
*Description:* Disease, often primarily of the liver, which is related to many other feline illnesses, causing yellowing of the membrane of the mouth, eye and skin.
*Treatment:* *, at once.

## Mange
*Description:* Parasitic infection of the skin leading to patchy baldness. Transmissible (in some forms to humans and other animals as well as to cats.)
*Treatment:* Isolate, and *. Seek vet's advice on preventative measures for other animals in household, and your physician's on your behalf, if necessary.

## Pneumonia
*Description:* Respiratory disease indicated by quick breathing and high temperature.
*Treatment:* *, immediately.

## Ringworm
*Description:* Fungal infection causing bare patches or a gray scurf-like deposit, transmissible to humans.
*Treatment:* Isolate and *. Seek vet's advice on preventative measures for other animals in household, and your physician's on your own behalf, if necessary.

*Right:* Hand-rearing newborn kittens. Like all very young creatures, they need to be kept warm (though not too warm). A hot-water bottle is a good source of this gentle warmth, as long as it's wrapped in a blanket.

*Left:* Not the easiest job in the world – but it can be done. With a bigger cat, though, an assistant to hold the patient would be essential.

As on the previous pages, the symbol * indicates that veterinary help should be sought.

## Botfly

*Description:* Maggots of the botfly, in summer, can hatch from eggs laid on the coat of a cat and burrow into the skin, causing swellings. (Parts of USA only.)

*Treatment:* Removal is tricky, * is advised.

## Fleas

*Description:* The most common parasite found on cats, detectable by small black specks of flea excreta found in the coat when grooming. Fleas can be passed to dogs and humans.

*Treatment:* Insecticide, applied on the advice of the vet. After an infestation, bedding and other articles and the immediate surroundings must be thoroughly disinfected. The presence of fleas must never be ignored, as they are used as an intermediary host by tapeworm larvae. Do not subscribe to the view that cat fleas are "nothing to worry about".

## Lice

*Description:* Cat lice, which are rare, are specific to cats – that is, they do not transfer to humans or other animals. The eggs are grayish-white, and adhere to the hair. When they hatch, the pinhead-sized yellowish-white lice spend their whole lives on the cat's skin.

*Treatment:* *, and burn or thoroughly disinfect all of the bedding.

## Maggots

*Description:* Various species of insects may occasionally lay eggs on the cat's coat, the maggots burrowing into the skin. Usually only found in aged or debilitated animals. If serious, *.

## Mites

*Description:* Cats are liable to carry a variety of mites, some of which are relatively harmless but others cause mange (see pages 166-7).

*Treatment:* If an infestation is suspected because of excessive scratching or skin lesions, fear the worst and *.

## Ticks

*Description:* Bloodsucking parasites which cling to the cat's skin. They are picked up in long grass and occasionally from sheep, usually on the head or ears but sometimes more widespread. Prolonged infestation causes debilitation.

*Treatment:* Dab with rubbing alcohol, used sparingly. This should loosen the tick sufficiently for it to be pulled away, but take care: if the head is left behind, it may cause an abscess. If you do not feel up to this slightly delicate operation, or in the case of a bad infestation, *.

## Worms

*Description:* **Round worms** look like lengths of thin white string, from 0.5-5 in (1.2-12 cm), which may appear in the motions or vomit. Frequent in kittens, but fairly easily treated. **Tape worms** affect adult cats, the characteristic warning sign being a huge appetite accompanied by a malnourished appearance. In the southern United States, **hookworms** and **whipworms**, thread-like worms about 0.5 in (1.2 cm) long, may infest the cat's gut, causing anemia. They will be revealed in the feces.

*Treatment:* Despite the wide availability of worming powders and tablets, veterinary treatment is generally preferred.

*Left:* Two cream Burmese kittens engage in mock battle. Kittens can be accidentally infected with round worms by their mother, but the infestation can be readily treated.

*Right:* Free-ranging cats like this one are much more prone to parasite infestation than those kept permanently indoors. But chewing grass is always an aid to good health!

If your cat has a serious illness, the vet is likely to keep it in his own nursing quarters until it is on the way to recovery, but there will be occasions when you have to provide nursing or convalescent facilities yourself.

Many of the precautions you need to take are a matter of commonsense, and apply equally to human convalescence. Your objectives are to prevent re-infection, to provide optimum conditions for recovery, and to make the patient's life as pleasant as possible in the meantime. You should provide a comfortable bed of easily-laundered materials, an even temperature both in the bed and in the sickroom generally, and complete protection from draughts.

It may be necessary to discourage the patient from moving about, and in this case a tallish box such as an empty cardboard wine case will provide a snug bed. Except in warm weather, keep a hand-hot water bottle under the bedding, remembering to renew it at intervals, and supplement heating with an electric convector or overhead infra-red heater if necessary. (Remember that the level of heat should be maintained throughout the night.)

*Above:* Sick cats need to be kept warm – though not quite as warm as the healthy red-and-white shown here, who had decided that the best bed in the house is on top of the boiler.

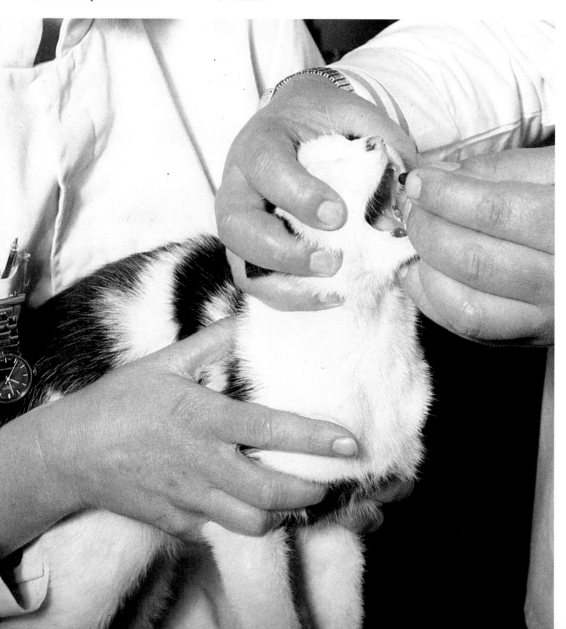

*Left:* The nursing procedure that most owners come to dread. When giving a cat a pill, it is best to follow the vet's example and have an assistant present to hold the patient still.

*Right:* Eardrops for a boarder in a quarantine cattery; again, it's a job for two. A substantial period of quarantine is imposed on animal immigrants to many countries (including the UK) to prevent the spread of disease, especially rabies.

## Interesting quarters

If possible, let the cat's nursing quarters be within sight and sound of interesting household goings-on – sick cats tend to retreat into themselves, and it is important to stimulate their interest in the outside world – but, of course, keep children reasonably quiet and don't let them worry the invalid. Until recovery is complete, do not let the cat out of doors; bolt the cat door.

If the cat has diarrhea or vomiting, frequent changes of bedding and possibly of the bed itself will be required, which is another point in favor of using cardboard boxes as nursing beds. Except where, as indicated on the previous pages, the burning of bedding is advised, it should be boiled in water containing a 1:50 solution of sodium hypochlorite, the kind of disinfectant used for baby bottles. (Seek a vet's or pharmacist's advice on a suitable commercial brand, as some brands have other ingredients which may be harmful.) Sodium hypochlorite may also be used, at double the strength given above, to disinfect wall and floor surfaces.

Note that most disinfectants and antiseptics used about the home are actually poisonous to cats. Unless the vet specifically recommends anything else, stick to sodium hypochlorite for bedding and surfaces, and 3 per cent (10 volumes) hydrogen peroxide (from a drug store) for the cat itself, for example when you are treating an abscess.

## Invalid diet

The diet of a sick cat presents problems, because while the owner's instinct is, quite correctly, to give light foods such as steamed fish and lightly scrambled eggs, this is not the time to expect a cat to take to unfamiliar items. The answer is to feed whatever, within reason, the cat will eat. Food which smells particularly appetizing – such as sardines or tuna – is worth trying, and so are the meat varieties of canned baby foods, and fish paste. It is better to offer food "little and often" rather than to stick to the normal mealtimes. Liver is best avoided.

If, despite all these delicacies, the cat still refuses to eat, there is no cause for alarm for a day or two, provided it takes water, milk (possibly diluted) or beef extract made up with boiling water and allowed to cool. In extreme cases, the vet may advise giving liquid food by mouth, using a plastic syringe; if so, get him to show you how.

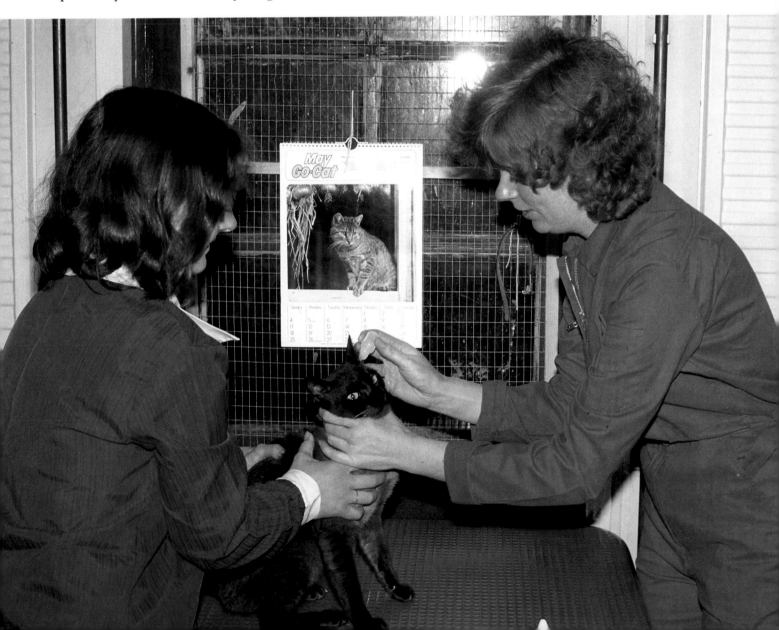

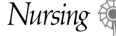

An overall and a pair of plastic or rubber gloves (plastic disposable gloves are preferable with infectious illnesses) should be worn when treating a sick cat, and when dealing with vomit, feces and soiled bedding and equipment. As in any sick-room, cleanliness is vital, but take note of the remarks on disinfectants on page 170-1. If it is possible, it is best for the handling of a sick cat to be confined to one person.

## Depression

One of the problems of nursing sick cats is that they are prone to extreme depression, and lose the will to recover. Spend as much time as you can spare with your cat, talking to it and stroking it gently, with great care, of course, in the case of abscesses or other skin or coat infections. Cats which cannot groom themselves may be sponged with a tissue or kitchen towel dipped into warm water and squeezed so that it is just damp. It is a good idea, if you have to spend time out of the sickroom, to have a radio playing quietly, tuned to a speech program. Energetic play should be avoided, but a favorite toy may be placed in the sick-bed for comfort.

## Force-feeding pills

It is extremely difficult to get cats to take tablets or liquid medicine, even when they are fit, but at least if medicine can be mixed with food there is some chance of success. This measure cannot be adopted with a cat that is hardly eating anything, and so the force-feeding of pills or liquid medicines cannot be avoided. If the vet gives you any of these to administer, ask for a demonstration of how to do it.

The easier way, which is not all that easy unless you have a knack of it or a vet's experience, is to have two people – one to restrain the cat and prevent its front paws from coming up in protest, the other to administer the pill. This is done by placing one hand over the cat's head, gently pressing at the sides of the mouth to open it and tilting the head back. Place the pill on the tongue as far back as possible, and hold the mouth closed, stroking the throat until the pill is swallowed. Do not underestimate a cat's ability to store a pill in its mouth until it can be spat out, and watch carefully for this for several minutes after you take your hand away.

The one-person method is similar, except that you turn the cat's head gently sideways, not upwards, before opening its mouth. This keeps you out of the way of protesting claws. But it is really only an emergency procedure, and the success rate is low, because an obstinate cat is more than a match for most lone nurses. If at all possible, recruit an assistant and go for the easier two-person method.

Liquid medicines for internal use are given by plastic syringe, using the same methods. Applying ear or eye drops is also better done by two people, and, again, let the vet show you how.

Unless you are used to it and the vet specifically advises it, the taking of a cat's temperature is better left to the professional. Again, two people are preferable to one. The thermometer is shaken down, lubricated with petroleum jelly or vegetable oil, and inserted gently into the anus. It should be left there for a couple of minutes. The normal temperature for cats is in the range 99.1°F (38°C) to 101.5°F (38.6°C).

*Right:* A vet's home visit for this Siamese and its owner.

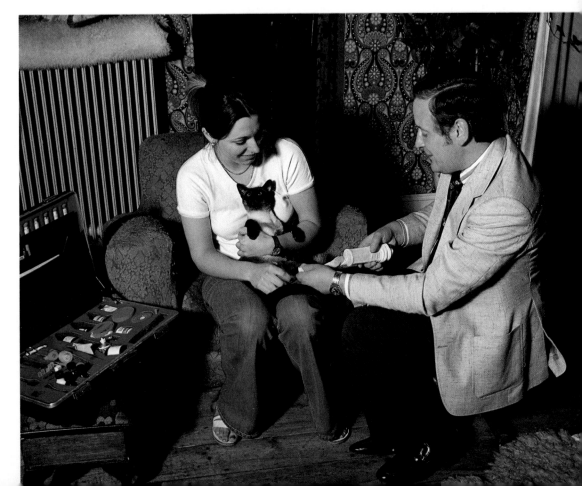

*Left:* The depths of the feline pupil. This calm and sparkling-eyed tabby-and-white is having an opthalmic examination.

First aid for an injured or poisoned cat should be regarded as emergency treatment only, with the object of relieving pain and supporting life while veterinary help is sought. In such emergencies, remember that local animal welfare organizations, or even the police, may be able to help if your own vet cannot be contacted. It is best for the owner, if possible, to stay with the cat while someone else does the telephoning.

**Shock** following an accident is indicated by apparent collapse, accompanied by rapid breathing and pulse, and a feeling of chill. Wrap the victim in a blanket or whatever is available – your own sweater, for example – and hold, preferably in your lap, with the head slightly lowered to increase blood circulation to the brain. Do not try to feed or give anything to drink. If you have to drive unaccompanied to the vet with a cat in a state of shock, place it in a box with bedding arranged so that the head is lowered.

**Artifical respiration** should be attempted by the amateur only in extreme emergency, if breathing has actually stopped. The "swinging the cat" method is the only safe one for use by amateurs. Grasp the cat by its back legs, facing towards you, and swing it between your opened legs to 90 degrees fore and aft, with a slight jerk at the end of each swing. Repeat half a dozen times. This method is particularly useful in cases of drowning, as the motion, apart from stimulating breathing, results in the ejection of water from the lungs.

**Heat stroke** in cats is most likely to be encountered during prolonged car travel in summer. Panting is the major symptom. Reduce the temperature with cold compresses, especially on the head, and seek a vet's help at once. Remember that a cat cage or travelling basket is a confined space and while you may be comfortable, the cat does not have the same access to fresh air and freedom to move. When travelling with a cat, make sure that the grille of the box or basket is in the airstream and that the whole container is kept in the shade.

**Fractures and dislocations** are usually the result of traffic accidents though, despite the cat's reputation for safe landings, they can result from falls or badly-timed leaps. Treat for shock if necessary, but do not waste time analyzing the injury; get the vet's help at once. The procedures for setting broken bones and dislocated limbs under anesthetic are similar to those in human medicine. Many owners who have been faced with the victim of a road accident have been amazed at the cat's recovery from what looked like very serious injuries; but if the vet advises that euthanasia is the most humane course you will have to accept his advice.

You may come across an unknown cat that has suffered injury, and if you are a true cat-lover you will give first aid and arrange veterinary treatment, and ask questions afterwards. Children are often the best sources of information on local pets, so asking any young passersby or enquiring at local schools could help establish the cat's ownership and identity. You should also report the matter to the police because, although road accidents involving cats are not legally notifiable in most countries, the owner may have left information at the police station. Any cat that is allowed outside will, at some time during its life, get involved in fights with other cats, or with dogs, and suffer injuries of some kind.

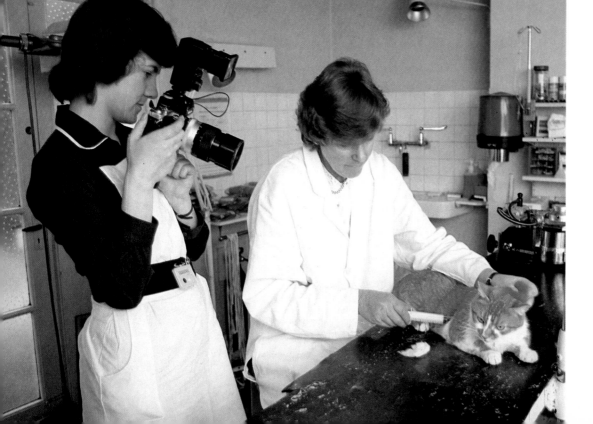

*Left:* A key point in the treatment of this domestic shorthair is recorded on film by the veterinarian's assistant.

*Right:* On the surgeon's table. The tabby patient, with the surgery nurse in attendance, lies unconscious while the vet prepares to operate.

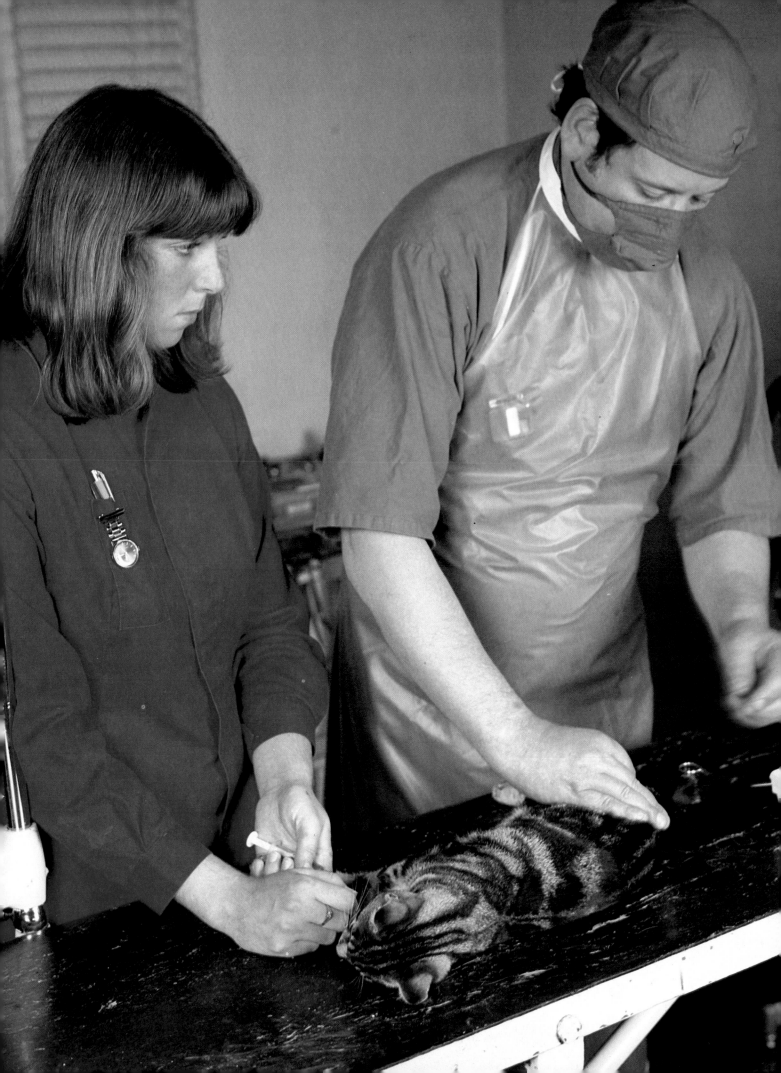

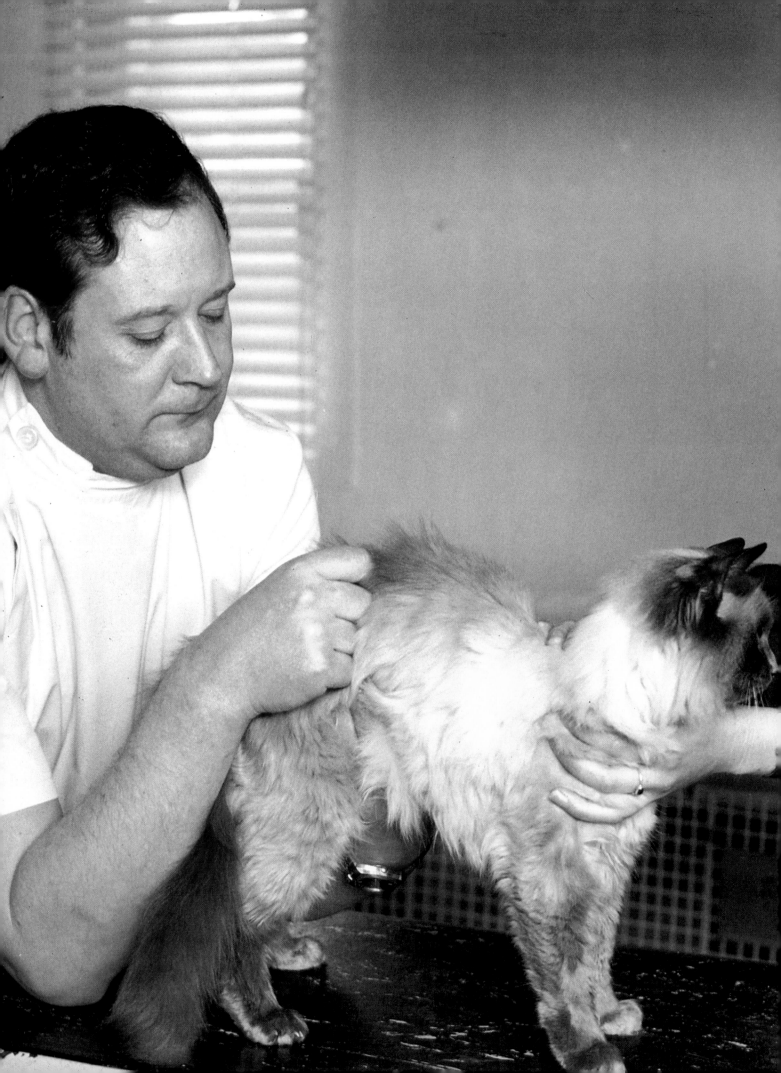

**Minor wounds** can normally be dealt with at home. Clean the wound with a salt solution or hydrogen peroxide. If it is severe enough to need to be covered, then you should take the cat to the vet.

**Severe wounds** resulting in serious bleeding call for more immediate veterinary attention. If direct finger pressure is not sufficient to stem the flow of blood, apply a pressure bandage or, in the most severe cases, a tourniquet should be tied tightly around the limb above the wound. Tourniquets must not be left unattended for more than a few minutes, the pressure being released momentarily at intervals in order to prevent gangrene.

Tell the vet, if you know, the cause of the wound, as he may need to take specific preventive action such as anti-rabies or anti-tetanus injections.

Puncture **bites** from rats or other cats are often hard to detect. The likely consequence is an abscess, which should be treated as described on page 164.

**Burns** are fairly rare in cats, and they are not often severe. They should be treated with a cold compress. Check for shock, and treat if necessary as described on page 174. **Electrical burns** are more serious, and not uncommon with kittens, which tend to play with exposed electric cables. For this reason, *never* use anything resembling an electric cable as a kitten's plaything. Typical electrical burns are to the mouth and sometimes the paws. Switch off and isolate the current (remove plug from socket or switch off at mains box) before touching the cat. Electrical burns are often immediately fatal. Very prompt veterinary treatment is otherwise necessary, with treatment as for shock (page 174) while waiting.

Cats are particularly prone to **poisoning**, partly because of the peculiarities of their digestive systems and also because of the attractions of rats and mice which may have eaten slow-acting poisons. The difficulty is that cats are susceptible to poisoning by a wide range of substances (including such common everyday ones as aspirin and most household disinfectants) and, of course, the grooming habit makes them vulnerable as they will try to lick away substances such as tar or creosote.

Cases of shock with no other apparent cause are likely to have been brought on by poisoning. Treat for shock (page 174) and get to the vet as quickly as possible. If you know, because you have seen the poisoning incident, what the poison is, tell the vet (or take a sample), but don't guess. Treatment for different poisons varies, and it is best to leave diagnosis in the vet's hands unless you are certain of the cause.

Because of the cat's susceptibility to poisoning, it is worth regularly checking the areas of the house where it is allowed to go to see that no potential poisons have been left in an accessible position. Make it a house rule always to close containers and store them high, preferably behind closed doors. Warn children about leaving model paints, photographic chemicals and other poisonous substances exposed.

*Left:* The vet ruffles up the patient's fur to examine the condition of its skin. A cat's dense coat can also conceal minor wounds.

*Right:* Cats' ears require regular checking to discover if any ear mites or other problems are present. For the professional examination shown here, a magnifier is used.

# 8 PREGNANCY AND BIRTH

Unlike some mammals which seem to regard pregnancy as a nuisance and are prone to drop their young casually, thereafter having little or nothing to do with them, queens are normally caring mothers and enjoy the experience of motherhood. They often purr between each birth, and will normally attend to the post-natal cleaning of the kitten, the cutting of the umbilical cord, and the disposal of the afterbirth. They usually need no guidance on feeding the litter, though in the case of a large number of kittens – say, six or seven – the owner may need to watch carefully to ensure that all get a fair deal.

Queens give their kittens basic survival training and teach them how to deal with their urine and feces. They even train them, to some extent, to get on with each other, discouraging over-rough play with a growl or simply by pulling the offender away. Nevertheless, it is a mistake to leave the queen and her litter alone on the grounds that they are self-sufficient and that "mother knows best". From about a week onwards, kittens should have the experience of being picked up and cuddled gently by their owners and others who will have contact with them. This includes children, who should, however, be warned to be gentle. From about four weeks, kittens should also be played with as often as possible (see pages 27 and 57). They need to gain social experience with humans as well as with their own kind, and in this way they will have both the security and protection given them by their mother during kittenhood and the experience to let them enjoy the pleasure of growing up as loved and cared-for domestic cats.

*Left:* Everything they could wish. The calico mother here is not just her kittens' natural source of food and comfort; she is also a perfect surface to play on.

By the time you have reached this stage in this book you will have decided whether you are going to go for a pedigree cat or a mongrel, male or female, neutered or entire. If you have ended up with an unspayed pedigree female, the chances are that you will plan a mating for her, whereas if she is a mongrel and is allowed out she will arrange matters for herself. These two pages are for owners in the first category.

## Oestrus cycle

The phase during which a queen may be successfully mated is called oestrus (popularly, "on heat", "in season" or "calling"). The oestrus cycle can begin as early as four or five months in some kittens, but the first mating should be delayed until about twelve months. Typical signs that oestrus is coming on are the "call", ranging from a quiet but repetitive cry in some queens to the full-blooded yowl of the Siamese, rolling on the ground, unusual displays of affection and unusually frequent urination. Oestrus itself lasts from seven to ten days, being cut short if the queen is mated. If the mating was unsuccessful, the oestrus symptoms will continue with greater vigor and insistence, and a housebound queen may well try to escape. Spraying and displays of bad temper are also fairly common.

Artificial light and central heating disturb the natural sequence of the oestrus cycle, and a domestic queen may be in oestrus at roughly three-week intervals almost throughout the year until mated.

Some owners prefer to let the queen go through oestrus once before her first mating, but if the queen comes into oestrus late (say, after ten months or so) it is usual to mate her right away. In preparation for taking her to stud, she should have a complete veterinary check-up, including a blood test for FeLV negative status. Vaccin-ation certificates must be up to date to cover the period of pregnancy and lactation – in other words, no boosters should be necessary for about four months from the date of mating.

## Stud males

For advice on a suitable stud male, you will need to consult someone with experience of breeding. Your vet is a possibility, and he may at least know a couple of useful names. Other possible sources of help are local cat clubs. You should visit any recommended stud, looking for a high standard of care and cleanliness, and you should, of course, agree on financial terms and arrange provisional dates with your final choice.

If you have a knowledgeable friend with breeding experience, take him or her along to help you make the best choice of male for your queen, bearing in mind whether you hope to produce simply pleasant, good-looking, healthy kittens or potential show champions. This really is a matter where experience counts, and the more you get to know your chosen breed and its variations of coat and eye color, the better.

When you deliver your queen in the first two days or so of oestrus – and you should always deliver rather than send her, if at all possible – you should take with you her vaccination and veterinary certificates, a copy of her pedigree and her diet sheet. Settle her in as you would into boarding kennels, and then leave her to it.

During your absence, typically the male will be allowed to mate with your queen about three times daily for two or three days. When you collect her, you should bring away with you a copy of the male's pedigree and, if provided, the stud owner's certificate of mating. Now, you have a wait of about three weeks to determine whether the mating has been successful.

*Right:* Six weeks old, and half way to being young cats. They can stand, walk, digest a little meat, and groom themselves – and, in spite of their startled expressions, they are always ready to play.

*Left:* Mother love. The kitten clasped in the front paws of this shaded silver Persian will one day be an ornament to his breed. But now he is just something for his mother to treasure.

The first signs of pregnancy, about three weeks after mating, are the enlargement and pink coloring of the nipples, combined with the lack of symptoms of the next oestrus. Like human mothers, queens normally look in the peak of condition during pregnancy, and there is no need to take special care of them. If you want confirmation of the pregnancy, don't attempt it yourself but go to a vet.

About the fourth week after mating there will probably be a slight increase in appetite, which should be indulged, and you should ensure that grass is available for the queen to chew. The appetite will continue to increase, and by the fifth week an additional meal will be necessary, evenly spaced between the normal two. This extra food could usefully be in the form of oily fish (sardines, mackerel, tuna) as constipation is quite common in the later stages of pregnancy and this will help alleviate it. Alternatively, the oil from the can may be given, together with a protein food such as baby cereal mixed with milk.

In the seventh week, the queen will begin to show the first signs of excitement at the coming event, with stretching and rolling body movements and a determined search for a suitable nest in which to have her litter. You are likely to discover her in open drawers or cupboards, or in other quiet, dark corners. It is time for you to prepare her kittening box.

## Confinement

If, up to now, you have allowed her out, you should confine her to the house lest she decides to nest in some out-of-the-way spot in the open. As always, pet stores have available all kinds of sophisticated and luxurious kittening boxes, but this is a case where, if you can dispose of the box and renew it without the slightest weighing of the cost, so much the better.

A cardboard box of about wine case size is ideal – but check that it has not contained such items as bleach,

detergent or other potentially poisonous or unsuitable goods. Cut a hole for easy access in one end, and provide a layer of crumpled (but not shredded) newspaper in the bottom. The top flaps of the box should be left in place so that the queen can have her kittens in private, but it is a good idea to cut a peephole so that you can check on progress without disturbing her. Have a similar box in reserve in case it is needed after the kittening.

## Siting the box

The box will be the base for the queen and kittens for the first month of their lives, so siting calls for some thought. As with the sickbed (but pregnancy and sickness are to be compared only in this one respect) the box should be within sight and sound of the household's activities but, so to speak, to one side of them. You will need to spend a good deal of time with the kittens during the first weeks of their lives, so consider your own convenience too.

You should, of course, choose a spot which is warm and at a constant temperature, and draught-free. The priority now is to persuade the queen that the box you have provided is the place where she is going to have her litter. Spend some time drawing her attention to it, showing her how to get in and out, demonstrating how the top flaps go down to make a cosy nest, and so on. Imagine yourself as a real estate man getting to work on a potential customer, and you'll get the idea.

As she moves into the last two weeks of pregnancy, the queen may need help with grooming – very gentle brushing – and you should check the nipples to see that they are free of encrustation, freeing them if necessary with a little vegetable oil. Check also that the anal area is not sore, sponging daily with warm water if necessary and applying a little oil. Now, somewhere between the 61st and 70th day of pregnancy, your queen's big moment, and yours, will come.

*Right:* There never was anything as ruffled, as tufted, or as densely furry as this langorous group of pedigree Persian kittens.

*Left:* A happy outcome to a carefully-planned mating almost three months ago. The points are invisible on these newborn Siamese kittens – although one tail has just begun to darken.

As the great day approaches, it is important to maintain the queen's interest in her kittening box and discourage her from finding an alternative. A sympathetic, gentle child can often be a useful watchdog at this time. Watch also for signs of constipation (vegetable oil can safely be fed up to one teaspoonful a day). As the time of birth draws near, the breasts and abdomen enlarge quite dramatically, the cat tends to seek out its owner for affection, and the appetite tends to decline or disappear. Try, if you can, to maintain a liquid intake.

The vast majority of births take place without drama, with complete satisfaction to all parties, and in total calm. It is important to remember this, while remaining on the watch for any possible difficulties. If the queen is in an environment of calm, she is more likely to have an easy time, so restrain children, if necessary clearing them out of the way. Confine other pets to quarters well away from the kittening box. During the onset of labor, sort out a selection of your favorite music, and make sure you have on hand all the items that you may need (see opposite).

### First-time mothers

First-time mothers will be quite confused and uncertain, and may need to be directed and re-directed to the box. More experienced queens tend to know what's what and settle down more calmly to await events. The first stage of labor, especially the first time, may sound fairly disturbing, with much growling and panting, and it may last up to 24 hours.

In the second stage, the queen goes into contractions which can quite clearly be seen. At this point, some queens want to be on their own, while others welcome the voice and touch of their owners. Respect their wishes, whatever they are, but stay within earshot. As delivery approaches, the rate of contractions increase to as many as two per minute, and the queen will find purchase points against which to strain.

Kittens arrive packaged in a membrane sac. Normally, the queen will lick this, and her abrasive tongue, combined with the struggles of the kitten, will break it, and the kitten will take its first breath. The queen will then nip the umbilical cord, clean up and eat the various bits and pieces, and lick the kitten dry.

## Help at delivery

It is only natural for owners to feel that they should help their pets at this time. Especially the first time – for cat or owner – this is understandable; what is going on will look as if it needs all the help it can get. But in fact, unless the queen is showing signs of distress – loud noise or great muscular activity, for example – all is best "left to nature". Provided the sac containing each kitten is delivered intact and then broken, there is no need for human intervention, which may be less than helpful.

But if the sac bursts during delivery, it may be necessary to help the kitten out, responding to the queen's contractions with a gentle pull, and resting in between. Such a birth may not trigger the queen's response to clean up, and you may have to do this yourself. Use kitchen towels to clean up the face, especially the mouth and nose, and body, and if necessary pre-sterilized sur-gical scissors to cut the umbilical cord. Do this about one inch from the kitten's body, and press the cut for a moment or so to prevent bleeding.

Labor is a relatively slow process. If, at any time in the early stages, it seems likely to be difficult, call your vet, and do so if, at the presentation stage, your cat seems to be in difficulty. But birth is not an illness; it is a perfectly normal and natural function, and the likelihood is that your queen will bear her litter with no problems at all, as millions of queens have done before.

The following items should be on hand at the start of labor:
Kitchen towels
Two hand towels
Sodium hypochlorite for sterilization and general disinfectant use
Absorbent cotton
Surgical scissors (new and sharp)
Hot water bottle
Polythene bags for disposal

*Below left:* The first seconds of independent life. The newborn kitten is a black-and-white, like its mother. It is already strongly active, though blind.

*Below:* Between births, the mother diligently cleans herself up. She will also clean her kittens as they are born, nipping through the umbilical cord.

After delivering a litter of healthy kittens, the queen asks nothing more than to be left to herself to feed them and relax from her labor. You should, of course, check that all the kittens are alive, healthy, not deformed, and getting their share of milk. Often, the queen herself will reject any deformed, weak or otherwise unviable kitten, and in this case you should ask the vet to call. But, as far as possible, let the queen enjoy the first week of motherhood alone with her brood.

The kittens' eyes will open within a week, give or take a day or so. They may need cleaning at this stage with a kitchen towel dipped in lukewarm water and squeezed nearly dry. It may be necessary to replace the box used for the birth. If the queen shows signs of moving house, take away the old box and provide a replica with fresh bedding.

At about 15 days, the kittens will start to explore their surroundings. A normal, good mother will keep an eye on them, hauling them back if they get too adventurous, but any stragglers shold be rounded up and gently re-

turned to the nest. At about 20 days, when the kittens can stand, weaning can begin. There is no magic about the date, and if you leave it for a few more days no harm will result.

## Weaning

Commercial milk substitutes specially formulated for kittens are available, but in general any milk form described as suitable for human babies will suffice. This should be given on its own at first, with a gradually increasing proportion of meaty baby foods and carefully-screened scraps of raw beef, steamed fish (boned), tender chicken (also boned), and so on. The aim is to build up to complete weaning at eight to ten weeks, giving three or four small meals per day, at the rate of one teaspoonful for each week of the kittens' age. Provide each kitten with a separate dish, and check any that steal from the others. Include the queen in the handout of tidbits.

You will be laying down the pattern of the kittens'

future eating habits, so vary the diet. Try raw egg yolk, a little scrambled egg, fragments of grated cheese, rabbit meat, and small portions of canned cat food. The greater the variety of taste and texture experiences introduced at this stage, the easier the adult cat will be to feed and care for.

Ideally, no kitten should be passed to another owner until it is three months old, fully-weaned and settled to an adult diet, and housebroken. By that time, it can also have been vaccinated. If you are selling a kitten or giving it away, it is up to you to ensure that you are sending it on to a happy life, fully equipped with the health protection it needs. It is a kindness to both kitten and the new owner if you send it on its way with an inspection by the vet.

Remember that even if the kittens are only the offspring of an encounter between your outdoor-life queen and an alley tom, you have a responsibility to find them good, caring homes. This demands effort, but such is the toll of kittens taken in on a whim and then discarded when the new owners are bored with them, that the challenge must be taken seriously.

*Left and below:* Kittens can start taking milky feeds after three weeks; after about five, they can have a little meat too. But they will go on nursing until they are eight weeks old.

*Right:* While kittens are small, the mother picks them up by the scruff. But the owner should always quickly support them under the legs and stomach, as seen here. Kittens must be handled gently.

# Summing up

And finally …

… The ownership of a cat is a partnership, in which you and your cat have equal stakes. It should be a source of joy to you both. To help you ensure that it will be, here are a few last reminders:

DO …
give your cat a regular daily routine it can rely on,
always provide water,
ensure that grass is available to chew,
give the cat somewhere to sharpen its claws,
provide an environment full of interest,
let sleeping cats lie,
talk to your cat, and listen for the response,
offer the occasional "treat",
remember that your cat has a life of its own to live …
… but let it share in the life of your own family.

DON'T …
leave your cat unattended overnight,
forget immunizations – and boosters – as they fall due,
feed your cat exclusively on dry food,
try to train or correct a cat by force,
allow anyone but a vet to put down unwanted kittens,
forget that cars are magnets to many cats – always check before you drive off,
laugh at a cat,
let children use your cat as a plaything,
neglect to watch your cat's weight,
mutilate it by declawing.

Remember that you are your cat's best friend, and the best gift you can give it is your time.

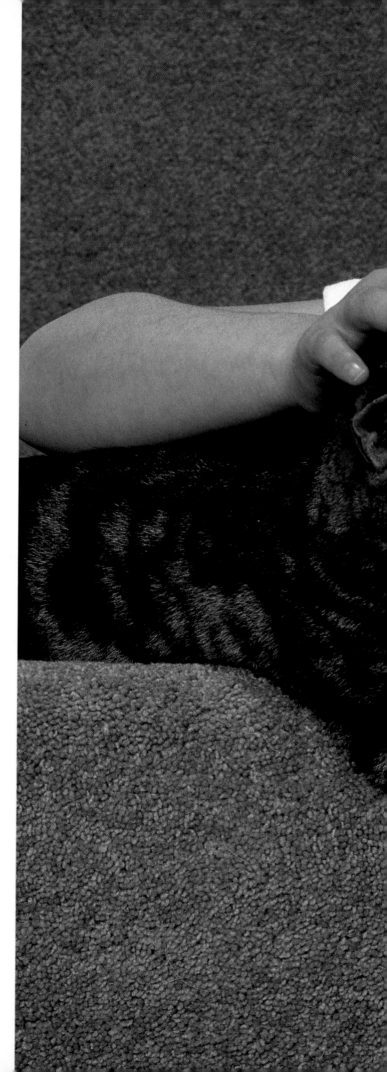

*Right:* Which of these two loves the other most? It's hard to tell. The young owner adores her beautiful tabby – but the tabby's expression is just as full of bliss.

# Index